MW01143891

WINNIE

Winnie

An English girl on the Prairies

Winifred E Bland

Edited by Chuck Grieve

MOSAÏQUEPRESS

Published by
MOSAÏQUE PRESS
6 Clarence Terrace
Warwick Street
Leamington Spa
CV32 5LD
www.mosaïquepress.co.uk

Copyright © 2008 Mosaïque Press

All rights reserved. No part of this publication
may be reproduced or utilised in any form or
by any means, electronic or mechanical,
including photocopying, recording or by any
information storage and retrieval system
without the permission in writing from
Mosaïque Press.

Cover artwork by Suzi Grieve

Printed in the UK by the MPG Books Group

ISBN 978-1-906852-01-6

Dedicated to the memory of
Sarah Rebecca and John Ellis Seddon

CONTENTS

Back cover: the author with her great-granddaughter
Kathy (Grieve) Broughton, about 1978.

FROM THE PREFACE TO THE FIRST EDITION

Over the years I've written parts as I've remembered them... Tom's girls used to say he and I should sit down and write notes on what we remembered of sod-bustin', but we never did.... You know it all happened, and there's still a lot could be added...

Fancy, figuring that it's seventy years this year since we came out. I can hardly believe it...

Let me know if you get this. I'd sure have a time to remember it all again! Love and God bless.

As ever,
'NAN'
Brandon, Manitoba
1 January 1978

Dear Charles I got thinking about
this one day so thought I'd write it
you may be able to use some of it
sometime, who knows

heavy
sleeves
bengy
rty
+
feng
boots

one thing its all true as I'm not
in my dotage yet, as I've
heard some folks say
Oh their old + yeust imagine th

_____ jum ocith coats. These were too
warm for Spring + summer we had cotton
dresses. It was very hot in summer + no trees
no shade only beside buildings. The men
all wore heavy overalls with straps over the
shoulders. But of course dark suits with
white shirt + tie for Sunday + dress up
Ladies long dresses, my long one had to be cut
so the batchlors would know I was young —
Fall 1902 We all had to have long undies
+ heavy coats, + woolen socks + scarfes.
The Moore's from Ontario had nice clothes
Jennie + I became great friends as they
just lived 1/2 mile East of to town say +
for a little while she + I were the only teen
age girls Our First Sunday there at Picks
we went to Moores for Methodist
service I believe Mr Moore took it
I know we did a lot of singing   over

Letters from Winnie, 1977

INTRODUCTION

IN 1908, JACK AND SALLY SEDDON AND THEIR FIVE CHILDREN packed their possessions into a trunk and joined a human tide of emigrants intent on settling the Canadian Prairies. Had they known what hardships lay ahead, there's a good chance they would have stayed in England. But they didn't and by hard work and a bit of luck they not only lived to tell the tale but one of them actually told it.

The unlikely story-teller was my grandmother, Winifred Elizabeth (Seddon) Bland. Much as she loved a good story, she never thought herself capable of writing one, much less of having it published – authors were educated people, she'd have said, and she was only an English girl who'd left school at Grade 5. Whatever she had to share, whether it was the sweet memory of springtime in Buckinghamshire or the sight of 'Winnie's gopher' running around without its tail, they were just 'silly little things' that had happened. Remembering them was one of life's pleasures, especially in her later years.

I had heard snippets of her stories as I was growing up, but when I started to take notice and ask questions, I was amazed at not just the clarity of her memory, but what she was remembering. As she told me about her early life on both sides of the Pond at the beginning of last century, it became obvious that behind this very proper elderly veneer was a person of considerable character and strength. It was an eye-opener. Here was someone of whom words like courageous, hardy, resourceful, loyal, respectful, caring, persevering – even adventurous – could be used, and all I'd ever been aware of was my old-fashioned 'Nan'.

A different kind of respect kicked in as the chronology of my grandmother's story unfolded: the childhood of measured happiness in England, the disruption caused by emigration to a raw wilderness and the fast-track to adulthood that awaited her there. The person I thought I knew – a person variously called Mum (definitely not a 'Mom'), Nanna, Winnie, Win, Betty and even, late in life, Auntie Canada – became like a montage of individuals, each a little different but all fascinating and delighted to have a newly interested listener.

That's how this book began in 1976. I was in England pursuing a writer's life, and she was in Canada happily providing me with raw material for my efforts. I can't remember what triggered it, but before long a voluminous correspondence was under way. It started with her child's diary of the actual trip across the Atlantic and into Saskatchewan and just expanded in all directions from there. I was fascinated. She was pleased I had completed a circle of some kind by returning to the old country and was enthusiastic about sharing insights about the way it used to be, on English attitudes and behaviour compared with Canadian, and opinions on the benefits or otherwise (usually otherwise) of new-fangled ideas.

Our letters became an extended interview by mail. I would ask questions or 'supplementals' based on her previous letter, or sparked by random thoughts, and she would respond with all she could remember, equally random. After all, seventy-odd years had passed.

It could be – and usually was – haphazard. At one point I thought I had a full picture of the emigration. "So when you left Kings Dyke for Saskatchewan..." I wrote. "No, we left from Calvert," she wrote back. "Where is Calvert?" I asked in the next letter. "It's in Buckinghamshire," she replied. "We lived there for three years before going to Canada. Haven't I told you about that? Well..." And a whole new chapter – new to me anyway – opened.

She liked using the blue 'airmails': self-contained letter forms sold by the post office that folded over themselves to create a protective wrapper around what you'd written. Space was limited. Her habit was to use every bit of it: down the margins and up the sides and even sometimes with afterthoughts encroaching on the gummed flaps. Deciphering one of these could be a challenge, especially as her writing was never the greatest and she often added extraneous explanations. As our project progressed, she took to using other scraps of paper, from notebooks or diaries or whatever she had handy.

Inevitably she repeated herself, but even this gave an insight into what she had seen and experienced all those years ago. She wrote three times about the homesteaders' fear of a prairie fire. In each case, the memory of a man on horseback shouting to Jim Peck to "grab your sacks and come on!" is followed by a description of the coyotes howling. An actual chronology, or simply the hard-wiring of her memory? Perhaps the two events had fused over many retellings until they had become a single reality.

My original plan, to somehow dramatise her story, was a non-starter. Instead, I realised as a journalist that it would make a good read just as she was telling it. As each letter careered between the many touchstones of her memory, so many pleasant afternoons were spent organising the story into a semblance of order that allowed it to sail its own course with a minimum of steering on my part.

When the manuscript was completed in 1978, my Dad had a few copies printed off at the neighbourhood Prontoprint. The five chapters that follow are that manuscript. It is perhaps inflating the currency to call that photocopied, stapled sheaf of A4 a first edition, but in hindsight it was. My grandmother liked the title *Memories of a Settler*, and that was how it went out to friends and relatives. Its distribution was surprisingly wide, as I discovered over the years when it reappeared from time to time in response to a question or an expression of curiosity. It was read with interest by an Iranian exile in Dubai, a near-contemporary whose own book chronicled an equally extraordinary life in Persia at the other end of the social scale. Successive years of schoolchildren in Thunder Bay listened wide-eyed when my sister-in-law read from the account of homesteading. When I started asking questions again in 2007, my aunt passed along the name of a distant cousin in England. "Speak to Trevor," she said. "He knows a lot about the family." He did – mostly from a dog-eared copy of *Memories of a Settler*.

For all its apparent honesty and attention to detail, my grandmother's manuscript leaves many questions unanswered. The most obvious and overwhelming one is why: why did they leave what to her seemed a happy life in England? Was emigration the success for their family that her parents, John and Sarah Seddon, had hoped it would be? What did life throw at the family after 1913, the date at which my grandmother chose to conclude her memoir? And then there are the revelations thrown up by modern genealogical research by another cousin, Barb (Seddon) Smith. "I think you'll find this interesting," she told me over coffee at the Keystone Centre in Brandon, Manitoba. How right she was.

In preparing this second edition to mark the centenary of the Seddon family's emigration, I have revisited many of the places in England and Canada that my grandmother would have known, dug into a few archives and trawled a lot of Web pages. I'm not sure what

INTRODUCTION

I hoped to find. Of course everything except a few church spires has changed so I also can't honestly say whether this looking and photographing and thinking deep thoughts added much to the story. What it did achieve was to restore links with family and friends and add a few I didn't know I had.

Inevitably, when checking memories against recorded facts as I have tried to do, some discrepancies come to light. I have chosen to footnote these where appropriate, or to highlight elaborating detail in extended captions to the photos, which are new to this edition and included, in many cases, for their historic content, not their quality as images. Minor non-invasive surgery has been carried out on the original text, mainly to eliminate repetition and incongruity.

In my grandmother's day, the written word was gospel among normal, decent people. If a sense of propriety, honour or shame dictated that something couldn't or shouldn't be discussed, it wasn't. There is much we can add today – hence the Epilogue, photos and illustrations. To rewrite the original manuscript, however, would have been to lose an element arguably as important as accuracy: my grandmother's voice. This is her story, told in her words.

I found the historical research fascinating, especially the personal dimension. Unfortunately once the bug bites, it gets under your skin, so the narrative is in danger of never being finished as new details, twists and interpretations enter the frame. At some point you have to draw a line, and as hardly anyone marks the hundred and first anniversary of anything, now is that point – just in time for Christmas. I think my grandmother would have liked that.

CG

Warwick, November 2008

15

English to the core

St Mary's Church and Church Street, Warmington, about 1900.

I WAS BORN IN 1893 IN A LITTLE THATCHED COTTAGE IN A village called Warmington, in Northamptonshire. Ours was one of three thatched cottages; an elderly bachelor lived in the middle one, and an elderly widow on the other end. The bachelor I remember as big and tall. Sally Brown, the lady in the other cottage, was little and she always wore a black lace bonnet with a big bow under her chin, and a black silk apron. Each cottage had a garden, and almost every garden in those days had its own soft fruit and mostly a plum, apple or more fruit trees. My father loved gardening, and taught me to love flowers as he did. We always had them in the garden, and as many indoors for winter as possible. My mother said I used to spend a good deal of time at the bottom of the garden. If she couldn't find Winnie, she'd say the child was probably under the gooseberry bushes having a feed. I don't remember that.

At that time, my father, John Seddon, drove the baker's rig. They used a horse and covered cart, and took the bread to the houses in a basket. He had gone to school in Warmington, where he lived with a great-uncle, John Ellis. Dad was good at so many things that he was always busy – in the garden, helping to build or decorate, and later when he worked at the brickworks, working alongside the clerks in the office on payday because he was especially good with figures. He could add up two columns of numbers at once. Years later, in Brandon, Dad was working for the Union Bank when they got their first adding machine. He returned from his rounds one day and saw it sitting there. "What's that?" he said. They told him, and right away he said, "I bet I can beat it." Well, they sat him down opposite the machine and started them both at the same time. I remember Dad coming home that day, as proud as anything. Dad always wished he could have been a teacher, and that was what I'd have liked to have been too.

Dad was born in 1869 in Liverpool. We always understood he was the eldest son of an Irish immigrant who had come to Liverpool with two brothers in about 1845, and who had married a young English woman named Ellis. But we learned that many years later from a woman in Canada who was a Seddon descended from one of the other brothers. Dad's parents – my grandparents – had died within a day or two of each other of diphtheria, and my father and his brothers and sister were taken by friends and relatives. My father was raised by his Grandmother Ellis in Warmington, and after her death, by John Ellis. Curiously, Dad's brothers, Tom and Daniel, and his sister, Lizzie, all had the surname Ellis. Dad was John Ellis Seddon. I never questioned this and never thought about it until later years.*

My cousin Nellie Ellis, who lived in Liverpool, remembered as a child having the grave of our grandparents pointed out to her. She said there was no readable name left on the grave then, and the church was destroyed in the last war. The graveyard now is a small recreation ground.

---

* The reasons might have been apparent if, like today, she'd had the benefit of public archives. Records show that both of John Ellis Seddon's parents were in fact English; the Irish association appears to be without foundation. However, it was his mother who was a Seddon, not his father. His father was Thomas Ellis, from Warmington in Northamptonshire, and his mother, Elizabeth Seddon, came from Liverpool. He was born before they married; his father was not named on the record of his birth but he was given both parents' names, as appears to have been the custom at the time. However the 1871 census identifies Thomas and Elizabeth Ellis as his parents. Records also confirm they did indeed die within six weeks of each other in the spring of 1878.

'Scholars' of Warmington, about 1880: John Ellis Seddon is the third child from the left in the middle row. He left school at the age of twelve.

Dad's brothers and sister may have been young enough when they were orphaned that they just used the name of the relatives who took them, or they may have been adopted.* It was common then for relatives to raise such children as their own or even to adopt some of the children of large families. My Aunt Edie and Uncle Bert would have liked to have adopted me. They had no children of their own, and I was allowed to go to Sheffield twice in school holidays to visit them, and to stay for a week or two. When Aunt Edie asked to let me stay with them, I remember what Dad replied. "If we had a dozen," he said, "we'd not part with one."

My mother was born Sarah Rebecca Sharp in Warmington on February 10, 1874. Grandad Sharp was a shepherd, but was too fond of the bottle. My mother said if it hadn't been for Grandma, they

---

* Barb (Seddon) Smith, in the course of her research into our family, discovered that Tom Ellis was raised by Henry and Sarah Millard in Liverpool, Daniel by the Joneses in nearby Bootle, and Lizzie by her grandparents, Alice and John Seddon.

John Ellis Seddon, aged twenty-two, and Sarah Rebecca Sharp, seventeen, in 1891, the year they were married. They were 'Jack and Sally' to everyone.

would have starved. I can remember my Gran Sharp only vaguely, and by a photo. Grandma Sharp got men's trousers from a factory and sewed in pockets and fly fronts, all by hand. She also did beautiful baby gowns by hand – she never had a sewing machine. Mum, the eldest, worked as a kitchen maid at a big farm, and her sister Edie, third eldest, was parlour maid at another farm in the village, so they could get lots of milk and eggs, which was a big help. Uncle Bill was the second eldest, and after Aunt Edie came Aunt Ethel, Uncle Newman – who became a groom to the Prince of Wales's Mounts and a real dapper fellow – Archie, and then twins, a boy and a girl. The girl died and the boy was Arnold who was crippled and could hardly talk. Her youngest brother, John Edwin, was just two years older than me.

Mum and Dad were both baptized, and Mum had been confirmed

by the time they were married on June 5, 1891. Dad was twenty-two; Mum, seventeen. Dad was a bell-ringer at the church, a respectful position and a duty which even now is taken very seriously.

We lived in Warmington until after I was three. I don't remember much of that period. Mum told me I went to start school when I turned three, as was the rule at the time, but apparently they sent me home saying they didn't take babies. "I'm not a baby," Mum said I cried, "I'm a big girl." I don't remember that.

Later, we used to go back for visits. When I was ten, I was a bridesmaid at the wedding of my Aunt Edie. We walked to the church, just the family and a couple of friends. We went through the village, without any show, and friends came to the doors of their homes and wished good luck. I think I just carried a prayer book. Aunt Edie had a blue dress and I was in white. After the service we went back home to Grandma and Grandad Sharp's for tea. There was no honeymoon.

Grandad Sharp was a lovely man when he was sober, and a very good shepherd. I have a photo of him in his cloth cap and big drooping moustaches, standing with his border collie beside a pen full of sheep. That's just how he was. He could direct his dog from a long way off just by whistling, and the dog would drive the sheep toward him. He sure loved his sheep. Often he would have a wee sick lamb wrapped in a blanket or old coat in a box in the kitchen. They were lovely to cuddle and hold on your knee and feed with a bottle. When we went for a visit we mostly had a feed of lamb's tails. They were kind of sweet and jelly-like, but they were supposed to be good for you.* We went for the day once or twice a year. It was only about twelve miles, and we could ride part way with the carrier.

Grandad moved one year to a farm at a small place called

---

* They had to be, judging by how bad they tasted. Cousin Mary (Sharp) Cuthbertson recalled a conversation with Winnie many years later. "She said they were horrible, but it was all they had to eat."

Barnwell, not far from Warmington. To get to his house, we had to cross a shallow brook on stepping stones, as the only crossing was far away and we walked, as one did in those days. Mum had my brother Ralph in a long dress and coat, and she slipped on the stones. But she didn't get Ralph wet; only her own feet.

Many years later in Brandon, Sam Gilder, whose father was our Gramp's best friend, said Grandad had a tonic for his sheep that he would never tell, and when he died, it died too. Sam said that as a boy, he and others would be hungry and would often go and eat 'Shep' Sharp's sheep lotus seeds.

IN 1897, WE MOVED TO KINGS DYKE, A HAMLET ABOUT TWELVE miles from Warmington in Cambridgeshire, where my father had a job with Itter's Brickworks. Mum's brother Bill worked there, and he and his wife, Sue, lived in Kings Dyke, which got its name from a huge dyke, or ditch nearby that we were told had been dug by King Canute as protection against Viking raiders. I remember going to the dyke only once. It was all green and some shrubs and trees grew in it. It was a beautiful spot.

Kings Dyke was forty houses each side of the main road between Peterborough and Whittlesey, built by Mr A Itter to house employees of his brickworks. It had a little grocery and confection shop at the top by the railway and later, a school, just across the road from us. Butchers' and bakers' rigs came two miles from Whittlesey once or twice a week. Market was at Whittlesey on Saturdays. I remember a big celebration was held there in 1902 for Edward's coronation; I still have the coronation mug that every child was given. The year before that, we had people yelling in the street: "The Queen is dead; long live the King."

We moved into No 28 and lived there for the next nine years.

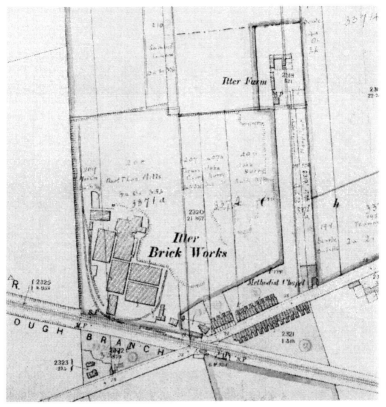

Kings Dyke: detail from 1901 Ordnance Survey map. The Peterborough branch railway line gave good access to London, ninety miles south, making the brickyard viable. The school was built beside the Methodist chapel.

Harold, Ralph and Doris were born there. The houses were simple brick two-storeys and all the front steps and window sills down both sides of the road were kept white. It did make the street look nice. Scrubbing the front of ours was one of my jobs on Saturday when I was older. Tom and I also had to clean the knives and forks – no stainless then – and the Sunday shoes, and I scrubbed the bricks of the patio at the back between our house and next door. I always got a penny for my work and Saturday afternoon usually walked to

Whittlesey to spend it. I mostly patronized the shop of Mr Rosher, whose son was a neighbour in Kings Dyke and later in Canada, as he gave a few more jelly beans or ju-jubes. Then I'd buy a halfpenny ball of crochet thread and walk home again.

On Saturdays, the road would be full of people pushing baby carriages and others on bikes going to Whittlesey market. A man called the carrier drove along the road with a horse and covered wagon with seats, and took people into Peterborough, four miles the other way, to shop or to go to the doctor or infirmary. The fare was no more than a penny a mile, I think, or maybe sixpence to Peterborough. On Saturday nights, our parents would walk to market at Whittlesey and there would be horse-drawn carriages on the road and often men and women on bikes. It was a busy and happy time.

Then on Sunday, Tom and I and others walked to Sunday school in Whittlesey, and went to service in the afternoon or evening. Almost every Sunday, we went to 'Grandma' Baxter's and stood around the

Kings Dyke level crossing, about 1906. A century later, the railway control office on the left is still there but no trace remains of the houses along Peterborough Road. (Photo courtesy of the Whittlesey Society)

The 1901 census sheds an interesting light on the Seddon household in Kings Dyke. It records the growing family of Sarah and John, whose occupation at the time was brickyard labourer. Interestingly, it also records that the Seddons boarded one of his workmates named Charles Wortherington. The next-door neighbours are Jim and Lillian Peck and their son, Willie, who would be instrumental in the Seddons' emigration to Saskatchewan seven years later.

organ and sang. There was no Church of England there, so Mum and Dad joined the Methodist church, as there was a small mission. At Whittlesey and Kings Dyke Sunday school we got prizes, and every year we had a day excursion to Yarmouth or Hunstanton or somewhere on the seaside. We went by train, with as many mums and dads as could come, and took food for a picnic. It sure was a grand treat, especially if it didn't rain.

We all had good gardens at Kings Dyke, with gooseberry and currant bushes, and mostly a fruit tree and hens, and there were allotments about half a mile away. We kept a pig and rabbits as well. When Mum cooked or smoked all she could of the pig, we always said the only thing left was the squeal – and it sure did!

Down a side road at the end of one row of houses, Mr Itter had a farm. We got milk there and I often stayed overnight with Annie Marshall who lived at the farm with her grandparents. They grew grain in the fields, and in the autumn we could go gleaning – picking up ears of grain left behind, to feed our hens. We loved doing that. Mr and Mrs Itter used to come in their lovely open coach behind two beautiful horses every two or three weeks to visit her parents, Mr and Mrs Marshall, at the farm. I couldn't go and stay with Annie those weekends.

Itter's Brickworks employed hundreds. As well as the tenants of all the houses, every day lots of men came to work on bicycles from Whittlesey and other surrounding small hamlets. Dad was a brick-burner – he fired one of the kilns – and helped in the office paying the men on payday. On top of that, he was a good carpenter, painter and paperer, trades he'd learned from scratch and enjoyed doing, so was always helping at these jobs.

Those were busy days for the brick trade. The brick-burners worked round the clock on twelve-hour shifts, changing shift every two weeks. As children, we loved to go and see Dad at work. The kilns were huge cone-shaped ovens standing in a row. They stacked 'green' bricks inside, then blocked up the door and lit the fire. The brick-burners had to watch the temperature carefully. On top of the kiln was a pot that could be lifted to look inside, or tilted a little to let some of the heat escape if it was getting too hot or when the bricks were baked. The brick-burners had long rods with an iron hook on

28

Arthur Werner Itter, pictured second left among other local worthies, 1904.
A Peterborough-born industrialist, Itter bought a disused brickyard in 1892
and founded the modern brickworks at Kings Dyke. Described as a bluff,
forceful and devout person, he took a conspicuous part in public life, build-
ing homes, a chapel and school for his workers and their families. He died
in 1910. (Photo courtesy the London Brick Company)

the end to lift up the pots. Sometimes they would open one and the
flames would shoot out. A ladder went up to the top, and sometimes
Dad would let us go up with him. I remember looking into the kiln
and seeing the flames down below just coming on. Some brick-burners took a chair to the top of the kilns, but it got very hot up there.

Sometimes we'd see them filling a cold kiln. That was where Uncle
Bill worked. He was a green brick runner: he filled a wheelbarrow
with a big load of green bricks and ran them into the kiln. I think
other men then stacked them very carefully in the kiln before the fire
was lit. We could see into the green kilns but not the hot; the flames
and heat were terrific.

Our Dad did not have a high wage, but it was a good steady wage and we were all clean and respectable. Everything was bought and paid for, and no bills were charged. We just lived quietly and had no debts.

AFTER HIS PARENTS DIED, MY FATHER HAD LOST CONTACT WITH his brothers and sister. Then, about 1898, he found them. I remember him coming in one day and saying, "I've found our Tom. He's in Liverpool." Tom had been taken by friends when they were orphaned. Through him, Dad found his other brother, Daniel, and Lizzie, who'd been the baby. In 1899, Tom married Nellie Robinson, the daughter of a Liverpool sea captain, and came to Kings Dyke where they lived next door to us in No 29. Their children Nellie and Richard were born there. Our kitchen door opened on one side of a brick patio and their's on the other. In later years, I sure got a surprise when I found out the actual date when they'd moved to Kings Dyke. I'd have been just six, yet I remember it so well. But they stayed only about two years. Uncle Tom found the work unsuitable; it was very heavy, so they returned to Liverpool where he became a stage hand. I think they preferred living in a big city, too. In 1908 on our way to Canada, when we stayed a few days with them, Uncle Tom got us in free to see a play called *The Sorrows of Satan*, but I don't remember much about it.

I was about eleven when Grandma Robinson, Aunt Nellie's mother, wrote to Mum asking if their daughter Katy ('aunt' to us children) could come to Kings Dyke, as the doctors had ordered her to the country for six weeks. Grandma Robinson would take Tom and me for that time. Liverpool! This did sound grand – until it came time to leave. However, we went on the train, and they made a big fuss over us. Such a big city and a lovely big house – the home of a sea captain on a passenger boat. Grandma Robinson's maiden sister 'Aunt' Ellen lived with them, and she seemed to take charge of

Winnie, her brother Tom and Grandma Robinson sat for 'Uncle' Tom during their stay in Liverpool in about 1904. The silk-fronted dress was her pride and joy until the other children branded her 'blue belly'.

us. One of their ideas – to keep us healthy, I guess – was to make us eat a huge prune every morning. Tom didn't like them and if he could he would tuck his in a pocket and later put it down the toilet. He was seven or eight then.

We were taken out every afternoon, to the beach, the museum, the art gallery or a big shop or to the pier to see the huge ships coming in. One day on the pier, I remember so well, was a small boy with a basket full of curious yellow fruit. They were small bananas, more curled than we get now, and smaller, but we'd never seen anything like them before. They were from the Canary Islands, we were told. Aunt Ellen bought one, but we didn't like it very much.

Two of Grandma Robinson's sons lived at home: 'Uncle' John and 'Uncle' Tom. They made a fuss of us children and were always bringing us little treats. Uncle Tom was apprenticed to a professional photographer in Liverpool city centre and took some photos of us, with Grandma Robinson, in our best clothes. I had had to have a new dress for going to Liverpool, and how I remember it! It was the first one I'd ever had that Mum hadn't made herself. We'd had it done by the dressmaker at Kings Dyke, who was Grandma Baxter's daughter. It was brown with fancy braid down the sleeves and a bright royal blue silk front, all shirred so it puffed out. The first time I saw my new dress, I remember thinking to myself, "Oh, this is pretty." I'd never liked new clothes before. But when I stepped outside in it, the kids in the street shouted, "Look at blue belly!" and I never liked that dress again.

Another son, 'Uncle' Dick, was in Japan and sent us picture postcards. It made me wish I could go there too. The women at Grandma Robinson's wore blouses of silk. Perhaps they'd been sent or brought home by Uncle Dick, but we wore cotton flannel, so we knew they were pretty well off. They even had a women come to help with the work, or for a party. The parties were mostly for young men. They were strict Baptists, and I believe Uncle John was a leader of a young men's group. Tom and I had to go to bed early, but we could hear a lot of it. It was all lovely but oh, did I get homesick. I worried that Mum or Dad might get sick. They had quite a large garden, high-fenced and brick-floored, where Tom and I could play. We were never allowed out on the street alone. They were very kind to us, but they were men and women and we, children. Although there were lots of pictures and books, there was not much for us to do. We were sorry in a way to leave, but it was a joy to be home and with Mum and Dad again and our own school friends. We were glad Aunt Katy was better and able to go home. Little Kings Dyke did seem good!

WHEN I WAS OLD ENOUGH, I WENT TO GIRLS SCHOOL IN Whittlesey. We walked to school, a crowd always together. It was lots of fun calling for others on the way, like my friend Annie at the farm half a mile on. The boys threw a ball or ran big hoops down the road and the girls skipped or played tag on the way. My friends Annie and Kate and I liked to just talk and look for flowers. On each side of the road was quite a ditch or dyke for water, and long grass. The dykes on the way to Whittlesey were always the best places for violets with the lovely perfume. Often a tramp would be sleeping in the grass by the road, or eating. Some would be pedlars who sold laces, buttons and thread door to door. We would hurry by as quietly as possible but we never had any trouble with them. Some would be friendly and chatter with us.

We lined up at school and marched into our room. At Whittlesey school we had long benches and desks to hold eight or ten children, I think. Later, at Kings Dyke, we had desks for two, with inset inkwells.

The school at Whittlesey was connected with the Church of England, although we had ordinary teachers, not nuns. I only remember one: a short, stout lady. Very often we were marched in twos to church. I didn't know why then, but it was for saints' days. We did our work with pencils on slates that you could rub off and use again. We all had our own pencil boxes. Later, we started to use ink and pens with nibs. You had to be careful not to get too much ink on the nib because otherwise it would splash.

Mr Itter got a school at Kings Dyke, just across the road from us, in 1904 and although I had only one year there, I loved it. Miss Lamb, the schoolmistress, was lovely. I used to go and help with the beginners, show them how to hold a pencil right, and to make threes – 'pot hooks' – and other simple numbers. I would always try to do my work

Kings Dyke School as it was in 1972 when Winnie returned to visit an old schoolmate. It was demolished with the rest of the hamlet in the 1980s and the cornerstones (inset) incorporated into a monument 'erected to commemorate the hamlet of Kings Dyke and the people who lived there 1897-1983'.

for the next day in advance so I could help. One of the things we learned was how to knit stockings, and our mothers bought what we made – in fact, they could say how many pairs they would need and we tried to make them. I also learned to crochet there.

After we moved to Buckinghamshire in 1906, I was again able to help. The school there was at Steeple Claydon, between Calvert, where Dad worked, and Planks Farm, where we first lived in that area. By that time I was in sixth and seventh form. I loved school; in fact, I would cry sometimes if I had to miss. If I did what I could of my own schoolwork the previous night, I could help Miss Cullis, the needlework teacher, with the little beginners. She was a lovely teacher. I hated to leave when we emigrated two years later.

'Knuckles' Reid was headmaster, a tall, skinny man and very strict. He had a long pointer and used it often. You had to sit for some classes with your arms folded behind, and if your knuckles did not show at each side, you got a rap with the pointer. We all had separate desks, but they had to be very close together as there was not enough room. The school was large. A big iron fence divided the playground – boys on one side, girls on the other – but with a nice flower bed along each side and roses on the fence. We had to drill outside every morning and march into school, and no whispering. We started with a hymn and bible reading here too, and then a big curtain was drawn to divide the room.

One thing I really liked was the flower-arranging duty. We bigger girls had to arrange the flowers in two large vases for the mantle at the sixth and seventh form end, and we could choose our own flowers. The Master's house was on the girls' side of the playground, and it had a lovely big garden with lots of flowers near it.

Every Monday and Wednesday afternoon was needlework. A door opened from our end into the sewing room. I learned drawn thread

'Knuckles' Reid and Standards 5, 6 and 7 at Steeple Claydon School, 1907. Winnie is seated second from the right in the front row; her friend Lily Feetham is third right.

work and embroidery here. Friday afternoon was singing. Mrs Reid was our singing teacher and instructor for our operetta, *HMS Pinafore*. I was just in the chorus, one of the cousins or aunts, but the preparation for it was a lot of work and fun. My best friend, Lillian Feetham, sewed the braid on the Admiral's uniform, and I on the Captain's. We had to stay after school several times to do this, quite late in fact, but Mrs Reid was very kind and would bring us some cake or a bun and a cup of cocoa.

Mr Reid took us two or three times a term on a nature hike past Planks Farm. It was always a lovely walk, and although he was strict in school, he was good and let us go and pick wild fruit and crab-apples. We went often to an old church* where Mr Reid pointed out damage caused by Cromwell and his men. Then we could sit and rest before walking the three or four miles back.

* All Saint's Church at Hillesden, just north of Steeple Claydon. The door with bullet holes blamed on Cromwell's soldiers remains an attraction to visitors.

36

Fox hunt day was special, too. We had to answer roll call, and then we had the day off and could go up to the fox meet. Most of the land around was owned by Sir Edward and Lady Verney; I guess he was the squire. They would always stop and talk to us children if they passed us on the way to school in the carriage and beautiful horses, and Lady Verney came and spoke at school sometimes and gave out prizes. I got a prize, which I still have, 'For good progress, Attendance, and Sewing'. We were very happy there and school was great.

WHEN WE WENT TO CALVERT IN 1906, DAD HAD AN AWFUL TIME finding a place for us to live. Like Kings Dyke, Calvert was largely built around Mr Itter's brickworks, but we couldn't get one of the houses provided for employees as none was vacant. So what Dad found was part of a huge old farm house about two miles the other side of Steeple Claydon, across fields and over stiles, and a good four or five miles from Calvert. It was called Planks Farm, and we had two large rooms, one above for bedrooms and one below to live in. We shared the house with an elderly couple, Bill Bailey and his wife, who had the back part and ran a laundry for the local gentry. He was tall and skinny and had a big hooked nose. His wife was small and quick as a flash. Old Bill fetched the laundry and carried it two miles over the paths and she washed it. You could hear her singing in a squeaky voice while she was rubbing away at her laundry: "Clear the darkened windows, open wide the doors, and let the blessed sunshine in." I used to watch her iron the maids' aprons and 'goffer-iron' the pleating on the caps.

Planks Farm was up on a hill, but to get there you had to go down another hill and cross two brooks and a meadow in between that often flooded. Both hills were planted to about halfway up. A plank walk actually crossed the brooks and the meadow, and although the footbridges both had side rails, the planks over the meadow had none. In the winter and spring when the water was high, the meadow flooded and covered the planks. They were treacherous. One time going home Tom fell in and I had a terrible time to get him out.

My Aunt Edie and Uncle Bert came to live at the farm for a few months. He was a scaffolder and was working at a castle nearby. One day Uncle Newman came too. He was smaller than any others of Mum's family and of course, being a groom to Royalty, he had to be a gentleman. He was a real dapper fellow with his gaiters and kid gloves and his cane. He wouldn't even take off his gloves to walk across the field.

I remember how huge that house was – it must have been someone's splendid country home once. It was a beautiful big building, with a slate roof, and there was a gravelled square in front and a long rolling lawn and a field with a footpath down to the two brooks. Two huge yew trees that were covered with red berries in the autumn stood in front. At the back were the stables, but they were empty and any traces of carriage tracks leading to the house were gone too.

At Planks Farm we used to go 'oodin' – 'wooding' – collecting twigs and dead wood from hedges for kindling. You could buy bundles of kindling, but this was much cheaper. I used to go with my brothers and friends off across the meadows from Planks Farm 'oodin' the hedges around all the fields. We'd come back with armloads.

In the spring the meadows and hills around there were blue with bluebells with long, long stems and beautiful delicate bells. And there were lots of what we called May trees – hawthorns with little bunches of white flowers that later developed into little red berries. You could eat the berries. At least we did.

WE MOVED FROM PLANKS FARM TO A HOUSE ON THE OUTSIDE of Steeple Claydon, and stayed there only about a few weeks before

Aunt Edie and Uncle Bert Stacey, 1906. Childless themselves, they took in Gilbert, the youngest of her brother John Edwin Sharp's children.

we got one of Mr Itter's houses. Thank goodness it wasn't any longer. The houses were in a row on a hill, with a pub at the bottom and another at the top. A dirty old guy we called Old Joe lived in an old streetcar at the back. He was supposed to have built those houses. They were poorly made; I think Dad said old lumber had been used. In storms the roof leaked and we had to scramble into Mum's bed and put pots and buckets down to catch the drops. If there was ever any lightning we had to turn all the mirrors to the wall, and knives, scissors, forks, anything metal had to be put away or covered. Everyone did that in those days.

We had a great big garden on the slope of the hill, between the house and the pub. At night when the pubs closed we could hear men yelling and rowing like they were standing right outside our door. Mum was scared silly of the drunks. Dad worked night shift for

Brickworks at Calvert, 1964. The site closed in 1991 and has been trans-formed into a pleasant housing estate whose history lives on in the names of some of its streets: Kiln Close, Brickhill Way, Clay Lane.

two weeks at a time. There were no locks on the doors, so Mum put a big box behind the front door, and a big dresser behind the door upstairs. It was a frightening experience.

But we weren't the only ones bothered by the noise. Outside the pub at the top of the hill they were just as bad, and the landlady, who lived above the pub, must have leaned out of her window in her nightcap and shouted at them dozens of times to be quiet and go home. Well, they would not be quiet, so one night she opened her window and instead of shouting, she emptied the chamber pot on their heads.

THAT HOUSE WAS AT THE OPPOSITE END OF STEEPLE CLAYDON from school, but still it was much nearer for Dad to get to work. We were only there a few weeks, until a house came vacant at Calvert. Calvert was a hamlet just off the main road to Aylesbury and Oxford.

There was a railway bridge with a station agent's house beside it and under the bridge, a small station. At the bottom of the hill, down a short road, were the five kilns of the brickyard and twenty houses for employees, beside a deep wood. By the station house was a small tin Church of England chapel which was still there when I went back to Calvert for a look almost seventy years later. I remember Reverend Pike came by bike from Aylesbury every two weeks to take the service there and Mum and Dad always had him come for tea after, at about 4pm. He had been a sea chaplain and we loved to listen to his stories about the places he'd been.*

On Saturday nights everything had to be put away ready for Sunday. We weren't allowed to do anything on Sunday except sit in the parlour and read, or go for walks. Every Sunday morning we walked to church at Steeple Claydon, children in groups and parents with prams, all very proper; we weren't allowed to run or play.

The woods at Calvert were alive with primroses and bluebells in the spring. One Sunday, after we got home from church and had lunch, Dad said, "Would you like to go for a walk in the wood this afternoon?" Of course I did, as we were never allowed to go through the woods near the brickworks on our own for fear of getting lost. We walked over a very rough path, all vines and ivy and brambles, and all at once we found ourselves in an opening about as big as an average modern backyard – golden with primroses. I just sat down and filled my pinafore. There were lots of bluebells too, but it couldn't match the dyke on the way to Whittlesey for violets.

Dad did the same work at Calvert as he had done at Kings Dyke,

* A letter from H Ferris Pike to the Seddons, dated 30 August and apparently written the summer after their emigration, survives. In it Reverend Pike writes, 'Remember me to Mrs Seddon and tell her I only wish I could drop in and have a cup of tea as I used to. I loved being there amongst you all. I hope Winnie and the others are keeping well and may God Bless and keep you all in your new home.'

and Buckinghamshire was our home for about two years. During that time, Mum went with a midwife to learn the ropes. In those days, a midwife came to your home to help deliver a baby. There was no trip to the hospital, and often a doctor wasn't even sent for unless complications set in. For Mum, it was invaluable experience, as we found out later in Saskatchewan.

EVERYWHERE IN ENGLAND AT THIS TIME THERE WERE POSTERS about Canada. 'Migrate to Canada', they read, 'The Land of Milk and Honey.' Get 164 acres free; build a home. There was even a song we used to sing going to school:

> There's a man, man, man in Manitoba,
> Saving and slaving,
> Building a nest,
> In the far, far West,
> For his own little English bride.

Little we knew of Manitoba!*

Jim Peck and his family had lived next door to us at No 29 in Kings Dyke for several years before emigrating to Saskatchewan** where they took up a homestead about four miles from Colonsay, near Saskatoon. The people who moved into No 29 after them were the Roshers. Ed Rosher had married Louise Roberts, from across the

---

* Or were likely to learn about it either, thanks largely to the Canadian government. Ottawa's effort around 1900 to populate the Prairies is well documented as a forerunner of the modern advertising campaign which pumps out a sanitised version of the truth. The posters she refers to painted a picture of Canada as a land of never-ending summer, bumper crops, happy and prosperous landowners, where the climate was 'invigorating' (never 'freezing') and the territory 'inexhaustible' (rather than 'desolate', as the Hudson's Bay Company had depicted it for centuries). A Canadian government website records that official publications eventually dropped references to snow and cold. As for Manitoba, its winter temperatures were withheld from publication abroad.

** Mildred (Peck) Haggard records in the Colonsay *Milestones and Memories (Vol 1)* that the Pecks actually emigrated to Hamiota, Manitoba, in 1903, moving to Saskatchewan in 1905.

road. They lived at No 29 for about two years, had two children, Grace and Frank, and then they went to Saskatchewan in 1907, and homesteaded near the Pecks. Then shortly after, Mr and Mrs Roberts, the parents of Mrs Rosher, also went to Canada and took up a homestead next to Roshers. A lot more from Kings Dyke went too, as we found out later.

We got many letters from the Pecks telling us to come. Don't worry about a thing, they said; they would look after everything for us. Mum was scared by the prospect of starting a new life. She knew no one but Mrs Peck and Mrs Rosher. I can understand better now just how much grit she had to have to leave her home and all her friends in England and survive on the prairie. She never went back to England. We kids were nervous too, but for us it was also exciting. Things like that are when you're a child. I remember being excited and frightened and sad to leave, and when my friends envied me, I would say, "Oh yes, but I'm scared." Half the time I wished we could stay. But we wouldn't have, even if we'd had a chance to change our minds, and Mum and Dad too realised it was for the best.

The hardest thing for me was to leave school. I loved it but I had to leave. That was the worst – saying goodbye to my friends and teachers. It hadn't been so long since we had left Kings Dyke, either. It was hard to pick up and leave for a new place, and then little more than a year later, to do it again. We were comfortable in England. Dad had a good job, we had a nice home; we weren't rich but we had no debts either. Dad wrote to the Pecks, asking if we could get a house, but always the answer was the same: Don't worry about a thing. So on March 19, 1908, after two or three days with Uncle Tom and Aunt Nellie in Liverpool, we boarded the *Corsican* and sailed for Canada. I was fourteen.

'Let's get off and walk'

The Seddon family: Liverpool, March 18, 1908, the day before they sailed to Canada. Seated surrounded by their children are Sarah and John – 'Sally and Jack' as they were universally known. The children from left are Tom, Doris, Harold, Ralph and Winnie. Standing are Jack's brother and sister-in-law, Tom and Nellie Ellis, and Nellie's mother, Grandma Robinson.

T HE FIRST TWO DAYS OUT OF LIVERPOOL ABOARD THE *Corsican* were good; we walked around the deck, watched the gulls diving to pick up food or garbage behind the boat. We watched whatever was going on, or we went below to lie down, or into the lounge to listen to music. The sea was calm and the ship's motion hardly noticeable, and we had no idea what was ahead, any of us. I started a diary to record our trip. Its opening pages – which read like a menu, I'm afraid, and give the impression we did nothing but eat – tell the story.

LIVERPOOL, THURSDAY, MARCH 19, 1908

WINIFRED SEDDON, AGE 14

We came out to the ship on a tender at half past eleven this morning. We boarded the *Corsican* which was lying out in the Mersey for 3rd class passengers. About 12 o'clock after 3rd class passengers were on, we went back to Liverpool for 1st and 2nd class passengers. While we were there we had dinner of boiled mutton, barley soup, carrots and potatoes with their skins on, then rice and apples. In the afternoon we spent part of the time in the sitting room and heard the Piano. For tea we had tinned beef, pickles, Damson jam, marmalade and tea. Our room is against the propellers so we woke several times during the night.

In the morning, Friday 20th, we came to Londonderry and stopped there about 6 hours for Irish passengers who came out on a tender. We had breakfast at 8:30 which was porridge, eggs, jam, marmalade, tea and coffee. We left Londonderry at 12 o'clock noon. Dinner was at 1 o'clock of ling fish, soup, beef, potatoes and bread, rice and prunes. A short time after dinner I began to feel very queer, I was sick and went to lay down. Later on in the evening Mother and all the children became sick, during the night we were all bad and did not get much rest.

Saturday 21st. In the morning the sea was very rough and we were all worse. None of us got up for breakfast but Father.

Our cabin on the *Corsican* was just big enough for two bunks against each wall, and we squeezed in our trunk. In those days, they put a family in a cabin together if they possibly could. That was why we had to go so low in the boat, to get a cabin big enough for all seven of us. Otherwise they put men and women in separate cabins. When I went back to England on my honeymoon in 1913, my husband Arthur was in a men's cabin and I was in a women's.

Once out into the Atlantic Ocean, the sea was very heavy and worsening. Most people on board were sick. Dad was one of the last men on the top deck on Saturday night before everyone was ordered below. He told us sailors in heavy oilskins were roping down the stairs and bailing water. The storm was at its worst. Dad said the waves were whipping up higher than the boat. "We'll never see morning, my gal," he told Mum. We all cried and hung onto them.

"Dad," cried Tom, "tell them to stop the boat and let's get off and walk."

It was so rough Dad roped the trunk to the bottom post of a bunk in our cabin. In the dining room, the dishes on the table were clattering and sliding from end to side to end. There were boards on the

'SS Corsican', from an Allan Line postcard, 1908.

edges to keep them from falling off. Some fell off and smashed anyway. We could not sleep – too scared and there was too much noise.
We were rolling and tossing all night. The next day, Sunday, we were
all so sick, but Dad went up for breakfast. Church service was held,
and Dad said the chaplain asked everyone to thank God we were
spared.

Dad heard afterwards that the *Corsican*, which belonged to the
Allan Line, was an old ship and in bad shape. This was its last Atlantic
trip.* We certainly thought it was going to be our last too, because the
storm continued, and as my diary shows, there were other discom-
forts to endure.

---

* Actually, the *Corsican* was a new ship although it is understandable that the conditions of the
Seddons' voyage would have made her seem otherwise. She was launched on the Clyde in 1907
and, with 208 first, 298 second and 1,000 third class berths, ideal for carrying immigrants to Canada
on the North Atlantic route, which she plied exclusively except for 'trooping' voyages during the
First World War. The ship's own *Titanic* moment occurred in 1912 when she hit an iceberg in the
Gulf of St Lawrence, sustaining only minor damage. She was not so lucky in 1923 when she ran
aground in fog off the tip of Newfoundland and sank. All onboard were saved.

Sunday 22nd. The sea was rougher, Father was sick and we were all in bed together.

Monday 23rd. The sea was so rough we did not travel much at all. The Chaplain on board said we were in a real hurricane.

Wednesday 25th. On Wednesday I did not get up but had a small piece of bread and butter and was sick after it.

Friday 27th. I went and had a little stew for breakfast. In the afternoon we had to go into the dining room where there were two doctors who we had to show our arms to and if anybody was not vaccinated they had to be then.

Saturday 28th. On Saturday evening we arrived in Halifax where we had to go off the ship with the doctor and three other gentlemen who asked many questions. On Saturday, the sea was calm and we went on deck. I caught a cold in my face and had an abscess under my tooth. Saturday night I did not get much sleep.

Sunday 29th. I lay in bed. My face was too bad to sleep or eat.

My abscess finally burst. All you could do with something like that was keep washing your mouth out with salt and water. I finally got the tooth out, but not there. Salt sure can sting.

We landed at St John, New Brunswick, on March 30. It was snowy and we had to pass doctors and immigration officers in what seemed like endless lines. Finally we got on the train and began what was to be a tiresome and slow journey west. We did board the train at a siding, I was later told, so my diary wasn't far off in thinking it looked like one.

We arrived at St John Monday 30th at 8 o'clock. We left the ship at 10. When we arrived it was snowing and we went into the waiting room to wait for the train. There is not any platform in St John. It is like a siding. You have to go up a few steps to get to the train.

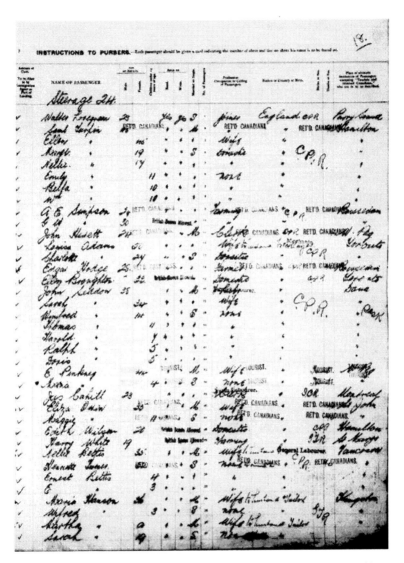

Fresh start: The official Canadian immigration record of the Seddons arrival in Canada, 1908. The document shows the family's final destination is Dana, Saskatchewan, via the CPR – another farming family to help open up the Canadian West. Just thirty-eight and thirty-four years old when they emigrated, Jack and Sally never returned to England.

The seats were padded and would not pull out to sleep on, and the carriage was heated with steam pipes. There was a stove in the end of the carriage where we had to boil the kettle.

We arrived in Montreal 31st Tuesday at 7 o'clock and got into another train at 10. The seats of this train were not padded. They were slats of wood and much harder to sleep on.

We arrived at Winnipeg April 2nd at 7 o'clock on Thursday evening and had to stay until April 3rd Friday evening at 6 o'clock. There did not seem to be much snow after we left Winnipeg. When the train stopped it made us laugh to see the people rushing out for refreshments. We had to go the rest of the journey from Winnipeg to Dana on the Canadian Northern Railway. The seats were padded but did not pull out to lay on (just slats). There was not a stove in this carriage so we did not get any hot water.

From Montreal, we rode in what they called Colonist rail cars. They were very uncomfortable and slow. The whole journey by train took five days, including the full day in the Winnipeg station waiting for our last connection to take us to Saskatchewan.

When we got on the train, Harold was sick and he looked bad. Mum kept him good and warm and when we finally got to Pecks', he had a rash and a big lump came up behind one ear. Then Willie Peck, their oldest boy, got sick and also had a rash. Mrs Peck and Mum realized it was scarlet fever, so they doctored them with old-fashioned medicine, as no doctor was near. A doctor at Elstow or Saskatoon later told them they were lucky they still had their boys, that only good care had saved them. As it was, it left Willie lame in one leg.

We arrived at Dana where we had booked to at 2:30 Saturday April 4th and we had to drive 25 miles in a sleigh over the snow. Our feet got very cold and when we got to a small Galician house we went in and had a cup of tea and warmed ourselves. The rest of the journey we did not feel so cold. It was getting dark and we could not see the house. But it had two rooms with a stove in each. We were glad when we reached our friends, for we were stiff and hungry.

Now my diary is finished and I wish good luck to everyone that reads it.

THE FIRST STEP MUM TOOK OUT OF THE TRAIN, SHE SLID DOWN a bank and Dad had to rescue her. It was twenty or twenty-five below, and Mr Peck was there with an open sleigh to take us to their homestead near Colonsay. He had straw and lots of blankets and buffalo robes in the sleigh, and we snuggled down and covered our heads

Dana station, about 1908 – an altogether more welcoming prospect in the summer than in April when the Seddons took their first steps on Saskatchewan soil. (Photo courtesy of Claudette Stevenson)

Railway line to Colonsay, March 2008.

with whatever we could. The house we stopped at was the halfway house, where Mr Peck changed back to his own horse to take us the rest of the way. While he did that, the lady made us tea. The floor of this house was earth and the woman was barefoot, but the tea was good and hot and we got warmed up.

Pecks' house had two rooms – a living room, a nice size with a stove and cupboards and table, and a bedroom. The bedroom was made of sod with a wood floor. Its walls were lined with buffalo robes or tenting or anything to keep the dirt up. The women and children slept in there, and the men on straw mattresses on the floor of the other room. Mr Peck's nephew and Mr S Templeton had come with us, and with the Pecks' four children and Seddons' five, it certainly was a full house.

Sunday, April 5, was our first morning at Pecks'. We all ate and got dressed for church. They had no toilet or outhouse; you had to go to the stable. Dad took Mum to the stable and coming back she pointed and said, "I didn't know they had another stable over there."

"That's the house," Dad said. Mum started to cry. Dad said, "If I had enough money, we'd go right back." I think he had five or ten dollars.

Sod-bustin'

A different picture: 'Dear Friend. Hope this finds you all well as we all are well. We are in Canada at last but don't like it much. We are getting on well as far as money goes. We get more here but it is all makeshift here and such a changeable climate.' The reverse side of the family portrait on page 46 which had been reproduced as postcards in the fashion of the time. Written by Sally Seddon. Undated but apparently written shortly after their arrival in Saskatchewan. The annotations top and bottom were added by Winnie in the 1970s.

SOD-BUSTIN'

W E DIDN'T TAKE MUCH HOUSEHOLD STUFF TO CANADA – seven people was enough, but Mum did pack her sewing machine. It was a table model and she wrapped it in the feather bed. She also brought a copper warming pan, and many times that winter in Colonsay we were glad to have it. Tom and I in later life could remember her putting red-hot coals in it to warm our beds. Mum also brought a silver teapot given her by friends in Calvert as a farewell gift, a large photo of Dad's parents, and a picture of a girl with daffodils, but we took nothing like fancy china. We left some beautiful things behind. We had no room. All of us had warm clothes, heavy coats and skirts and blouses, and the men had heavy shirts and underwear, but the first things we had to buy, I remember, were felt boots. Our feet almost froze in our good English leather ones.

I had a long skirt, to be a grown-up, as we knew I would have to go to work when we got there. But when we arrived, Mrs Peck said, "You'd better cut that girl's skirt – it's all bachelors here and they'll all be thinking she's a woman. Besides, there's no work here anyway." Was I ever glad to get it cut down.

Mum had made or bought new woollen undies for all the boys before we left England. When we got to Pecks', they were all near crazy with itching. Mum and Mrs Peck found they had body lice – great big ones. They boiled the underwear and put it out to freeze; it froze solid as iron, but there still some 'cooties'. They had to burn the underwear finally.

Our plan all along had been to take up a homestead in Saskatchewan, just as the Pecks and Roshers had done. But Dad found that the only land left was too stony and hilly, and he had no money to buy things for farming.

So he got work on the Canadian Pacific Railway section at Elstow, laying tracks. He walked home from work on Saturday night and back again on Sunday. Pecks' farm was about midway between Colonsay and Elstow – four miles from each. We stayed with them six weeks or two months. We were going to move to Elstow but Mr Moore, who lived near Colonsay, and two others coaxed Dad to stay at Colonsay as our three boys – Tom, Harold and Ralph – and four-year-old Doris made up the number of children in the township to get a school. I was too old.

THAT SPRING AT PECKS' WAS SOME EXPERIENCE. THE FIRST TIME we heard the coyotes howl sure was terrifying. It became a regular thing to listen to them. Sometimes they sounded quite close to the house, too, but they always stayed back in the bush or went to the farms looking for food. We never saw them, except far off on the top of high ground, silhouetted against the sky, but guns were always ready at hand anyway. I never heard of Dad's being afraid of meeting any animal as he walked home along the tracks on Saturday nights, or of ever seeing any.

The one wild animal we did see a lot of was the gopher. The ground was alive with them. We spent hours trying to catch them. One boy put one of the little round tubes that yeast cakes came in down a hole and a gopher coming out got its front feet and head caught and skittered around for hours half-stuck in this tube. The baby gophers were so cute, and I always wanted to catch them. One day I did manage to get hold of one, but only by the tail. To my surprise, the wee thing scooted off and left its tail in my hand! We watched that one a long time. It was always 'Winnie's gopher'.

In the spring, we saw flocks of ducks, geese and white turkeys flying over, and once in a while you might see a chicken hawk trying to get a chicken. We had plenty of buffalo wallows, but the first buffalo I saw was at the Brandon Fair. That was where I first saw Indians, too.

Saskatchewan was real bald-eyed prairie – not a tree in sight, only small bushes and wolf willow, which grew in silvery-leafed clumps no higher than four or five feet. There were wild violets when the snow went, and lots of delicious wild strawberries, lovely fresh, or preserved – if any were left!

Pecks had one real old horse, called Fred, that they left at home for any use that might come up. He took us to Longstaff, four miles away, on the stone boat – just runners with boards across them about ten inches from the ground. You could sit on the stone boat or walk alongside, and either way it took hours to get anywhere. Oxen were used too, but they were just as slow, and the stone boat wasn't very comfortable, especially on rocky ground. I rode on it, but I sure got some bumps.

One afternoon in April, we saw a cloud of smoke in the distance. Prairie fire! A man came galloping into the yard. "Get your broom and sacks, Jim, and come on!" the man shouted without getting off his horse. As many men as could grabbed sacks and went. There was a lot of smoke, and at night it was an arch of light spreading across the horizon, like a brilliant sunset. We could see the flames licking at the sky. One of the boys got busy and ploughed a fire guard around the house right away, but fortunately the fire didn't come that close before it was put out.

WITH ONLY TWO ROOMS, PECKS' HOUSE WAS PACKED. IN THE sod-walled bedroom were the beds for the women and girls – springs were bare boards. For the men and boys, big ticks filled with straw were made into beds on the floor of the other room. We carried them out each night, and put them on top of the other beds during the day.

Mr Peck and three other men loaned Dad money for wood and materials to build a two-room shack of our own in Colonsay. In May, we held a 'bee' to build it, and with all the available men helping, it was soon up. There was only one other shack there before ours, belonging to Mr Jefferies who had the livery stable – two horses and a cart. Goyette's general store, the blacksmith and the Beaver Lumber yard run by George King were the only other buildings. Mr Jefferies and Mr Goyette told Dad where to build. There was a town planned at Colonsay, and although streets hadn't been marked out, they knew where things were supposed to go. When they built the church near us, they left room for the street in between.

So, one Saturday in May 1908, after about six weeks with our friends, Mum and us children went into Colonsay to stay, to be there when Dad came home from work at Elstow. We couldn't get a cup of tea until he came, because he was bringing the stove pipe, and the stove smoked so without it. We went into the house and got it cleaned up. We had ticking all made for the two bunk beds, and a large one for Mum and Dad's, and Pecks brought some hay. We filled the two for the bunks and sewed them up, and then, laughing, all helped carry them into the bedroom. Well, they were so full the bottom one touched the top bunk. It was a huge joke. We all pressed down, but up it came. Then one or two of the boys got inside – and it sprang back again. What fun! But it was getting to ten or eleven o'clock, and no Dad or chimney pipe. Mum and I were starting to worry. We unstitched the ticks and took a lot of the hay out, and final-

Mrs Peck poses with five of her children in front of the family home, about 1908. This is the sod house, measuring about four metres by nine metres, that the Seddons shared for about six weeks while their own house was being built. (Photo courtesy of Colonsay History Book committee)

ly got the children to bed, two in each bunk, and got the big tick filled. Midnight, and he still wasn't there. Finally, about 1am, we heard some whistling – our Dad. So, while Mum and I held the lantern, Dad sawed a hole in the roof and we finally got the chimney up. Then we lit the fire and made a cup of tea.

I don't know what the measurements of our shack were, but the cook stove was in the middle and when we were cooking in the summer the whole room was like an oven. Our shack was all bare studs. For the outside there was one ply of planks, then a layer of tar paper, then the outer covering of siding boards. One of the living room windows was beside the door, facing south; the other was in the west side. The bedroom opened off the living room opposite the front door, in the middle of the north end, and had one window, looking north. Ice built up on the inside of the bedroom walls in winter because it was unheated except for what warmth came in from the other room. The bedroom was about eight or nine feet long, as Mum and Dad's bed on one side – a spring on boards – was six feet and left a small space at the end to hang clothes behind a curtain. Two bunk beds, made of slats of wood on frames, were on the other side of the room, and a small table Dad made sat under the window. In the middle was our big packing case, used as a table, with the lamp on it.

We also had a dug-out cellar, maybe eight feet square and about six feet or so deep. You got to it through a trap door in the floor and down a ladder Dad made. He also made boxes to keep things in down there. It all had to be air-tight. The cellar walls were plain earth – no wood on the walls or floor – and it was always cold.

Dad was a good carpenter, and made the furniture for the living room. He built a big long table under the window on the south side and one stationary bench fastened to the wall. A moveable bench was on the other side. This could seat ten or twelve, and Dad also made several stools that could be slipped under the table. He built shelves on the west wall for groceries and supplies. We had a big round barrel thing to hold the bread. The floor was made of boards, and we finally got linoleum on it, which was a help when muddy feet came in.

Our drinking and cooking water that first summer Mr Jefferies had to haul from twenty miles away, but wells were dug the next year. For washing we used water from the CPR pumping station. It was too alkaline to drink. In the winter we melted snow. The winter of 1908 we burned only wood in the stove. The men had to fetch it from the bush at Dana, twenty-five miles away.

When we first moved into our little house, Mr Goyette had a sign up in his grocery store. 'No credit, please don't ask,' it said. As Dad knew the grocer at Elstow, Mr Peck took him and they got groceries and things we needed. Then on Saturday night, Dad walked the eight miles home along the CPR tracks carrying groceries. When Mr Goyette heard that, he changed his tune, came over to see Dad and told him he could get anything he needed and pay at the months' end. Everybody knew that one garnishment of wages with the CPR, over bills owing, meant a loss of job.

OUR FIRST SUNDAY AT PECKS' WE WENT TO MR AND MRS Moore's home, five miles from Pecks', for a Methodist service. I think Mr Moore took the service, and I know we did a lot of singing. Moores' home was very nice and cosy – living room, dining room and a large lean-on kitchen, and two bedrooms upstairs. It was more like England. I liked it! They had a piano and Mrs Moore and Jennie played. They made us feel very welcome, and Jennie became a great friend. They lived half a mile east of Colonsay, on the other side of a low hill and a valley full of buffalo wallows. There were eighteen or twenty of them. You could just imagine buffalo lying down in them and kicking around in the dust. Of course there were no buffalo there any more, and the wallows were a mass of wild strawberries in the spring.

That first spring we went to Moores' for Sunday school too. Mr Moore was the superintendent; my teacher was Mrs Urquart. A little later, after we had moved into Colonsay, an Anglican student named Mr Whiting came and held services in the Beaver Lumber shed, and plans were started for building an Anglican church. One Sunday in June it rained and the roof of the shed leaked. It was too full of lumber anyway, so Mum sent word for them to come and hold the service in our shack. The men carried planks and nail kegs over to make seats, because Dad hadn't finished ours yet, and the children sat on the floor. Our little house was packed.

Services were held regularly after that in our shack. Average attendance was nine, but it grew in a few weeks. The first Anglican communion was held in our shack too. Reverend Lloyd came on the day of the dedication of the Elstow church. The packing case Dad had made for coming over from England was covered with a white linen cloth and used for an altar, and a red cloth was placed over the stove for a pulpit. It was a grand service. The shack was full.

About June or July 1908, Mr and Mrs Peebles started work on their boarding house in Colonsay, and Sid Smith put up a butcher shop. The CPR was building lines all over. Dad was one of the men who laid the steel from Colonsay to Elstow. But as soon as men were put on the Colonsay section, Dad got on there. Soon work was also under way on a section house. I remember the day in June when the first passenger train came through, all decked with flags and greenery. We didn't get a station until 1909.

AS OUR THREE BOYS AND DORIS MADE UP THE QUOTA OF twelve for a school, it wasn't long before the lumber for it was ready and a bee was held to put it up. That was early in June, I think. We all hammered a few nails in. The school was ready in October, and Miss King came from the East to teach. She lived with her parents, grandmother and brother, Bert, on their farm about four miles south-east.

Another bee was held in the autumn, after the school was finished, to start the Anglican church. Money to pay for it was raised through box socials, picnics and concerts. As soon as harvest was over and the men were free, work started. Mr King, two Shier men, Mr Chase and all helped, and Dad spent every minute he could on it. We all helped where we could, putting in a few nails, especially when lathing was being done. The shell was up before the hard frost came. When we started using the church, Dad lit the first fire in the big heater, and after that he or Tom would get it warm for cleaning and for Sundays.

Work on it was rather slow because it was all voluntary. Mr Whiting

Colonsay's first school, 1908. The Seddons' four youngest children made up the quota of twelve to qualify for a school in the community.

worked hard to get it paid for. He lived in Elstow, and with Viscount parish as well, had three to attend to. The first service was held in the spring of 1909 in just a shell with planks across nail kegs for seats. Mum and I and some others who loved to sing sat together, like a choir. Later in the spring, Reverend Lloyd came to dedicate it, and took as the text for his sermon the passage in Deuteronomy where God told Moses to plough and sow, a little here and a little there. The church wasn't plastered, nor had seats when we left a year later, but services were held regularly from that first spring. In 1909, quite a lot of new settlers came, and a Sunday school was started too.

Life on the prairie

Mr and Mrs Jim Peck at Colonsay, 1915.

SUMMER WAS THE SEASON FOR PICNICS – HUGE PICNICS, with folks from miles around whom we didn't even know. It was a big social occasion. Everybody brought their own lunch, and tea was provided. There were games, such as egg and spoon, where you tried to run as far as you could in a roped-in space without dropping the egg off your spoon. It was mostly women in that one, but there were three-legged races and sack races for men, women and children, and sometimes people played horseshoes and baseball. Our team played the teams from Elstow and Viscount. By 1909, we had quite a team, too.

Big logs were pulled in to sit on, if you wished, and the girls would watch and cheer for our team. At first it was just Jennie Moore, Eunice Longstaff and me, but later two more girls came in with their brothers and we had four or five 'boosters'. We watched the game and cheered, and the bachelors sat with their arms around us. Fred Rosher was always there to help and play and tease the girls, and Pete Ingham, who lived half a mile west of town, was another real sport, and always had his arms around the girls.

Then there were the box socials. Summer and winter, they were always popular and like picnics, a good way to raise money for the church. The women made them up, mostly out of shoe boxes, and decorated them with pretty coloured crepe paper, each trying to do the best. The bachelors all wanted to know whose boxes they were.

Some of the boxes were beautifully decorated; some were made into beautiful baskets, while others were more simply decorated. Each married man would try to get another woman's, and of course the bachelors tried to find out the boxes packed by their 'special one'.

In the winter, these socials were held in the school, with everyone sitting at the desks. The boxes were brought in wrapped, and someone who knew nothing about them put them all on a table in front. Most of the ladies were wonderful cooks and the box would usually have sandwiches, cake, cookies, some fancy pie, and most had some homemade candy. It was supposed to be enough for two. The men bid on the boxes, and you sat and ate with whoever bought your box. Fifty cents was a good price. The auction was always exciting; some went sky-high if a couple of bachelors thought it was the one they wanted. Sometimes they got fooled!

Mostly the box socials had a short program: a solo or a reading, or violin and piano playing; sometimes a short skit. We had lots of fun at them, and they were important parts of our social life, especially in winter – a Christmas social was held in 1908 too – but one or two of the bachelors we shunned. There was never any real trouble with them, but I remember in the spring of 1909 one bachelor got his sister-in-law in what we used to call the 'family way', and disappeared before the men could tar and feather him. They would have, too!

The Sunday school was well-established by that Christmas and a children's concert was put on. Some sang a few verses or performed a small play. I was in a skit about a milkmaid. The boys had a small skit too, after tea and refreshments, which our mothers provided. Tea was always supplied at social occasions. The Sunday school superintendent was Mr Moore, and Mrs Moore and Mum were teachers, as were Mr and Mrs Urquart, who came from Ontario with their four girls, and Mrs Smith, the butcher's wife, a little English lady whom we all liked

Colonsay's St Matthias Anglican Church, March 2008. The chancel and bell tower predate the surrounding trees by many years.

and who was always willing to bake and help at socials. Miss King, the school teacher, a dainty little thing we liked so much, was instructress. She even tried to teach my brother Tom to skate the first winter, with skates clamped on his shoes, but she finally gave up because Tom kept bumping into her and knocking her down too.

Tom was eleven the year we emigrated and was often into mischief, at school or at home or anywhere. He was always doing something to tease somebody, and of course he always got blamed whether he did it or not. Miss King must have often wondered what he would be up to next. One day at school, for a surprise for teacher, he caught a gopher and put a string around its neck. I don't know how he did it, but what a surprise!

"Tom Seddon," said Miss King, "come to the front of the room." He got the strap.

That winter Tom or Dad always lit the stove in the school, and one morning after Tom had lit it, the strap was missing – he had decided it could go on as kindling, and cut it up and put it in the fire. I can't remember if another one was ever bought or not.

At Pecks' one Sunday morning, when the boys were playing outside, Tom pushed Harold in the face and Dad took out the strap. As soon as the dog saw it, he beat a path outside and wouldn't come back until the strap was put away. But Tom still got it.

One day an old bachelor came and asked if Tom could go and drive the oxen while he drove the plough. Tom went with Mr Lane, but after they'd started working, the old fellow started swearing and Tom didn't know if it was at the oxen or him, so he left and walked four miles home. It must have been the oxen, because he went back, but he was pretty scared of the old guy.

Tom helped him cut wheat, driving the oxen by poking them with a rake handle with a big spike sticking out of it. One yoke of oxen, a horse and a cow was all the livestock Mr Lane had. One of Tom's jobs was putting the oxen in the barn and feeding them. As he was taking the hay up to them one day, one of them swung its head and knocked the wind out of Tom with the brass knob on the end of its horn. Something was always happening to Tom.

Harold and Ralph were still quite young then, and mostly just played around with the other children. At first there weren't many other boys around, just the one Jeffrey boy. They played on the prairie and chased gophers. Doris, at four, stayed closer around the house, but the boys didn't go far away because there wasn't anywhere for them to go.

Colonsay had the most gorgeous sunsets. Oh, they were beautiful! But if it thundered and lightninged, the black clouds rolled across the prairie like a big black wave, drowning out everything else.

I remember how hot the first summer seemed to be. There were no trees and no shade except beside buildings. We wore cotton dresses. The men all wore heavy overalls with straps over the shoulders all week, but of course dark suits with white shirt and tie for Sunday and dress-up, and for the women, long dresses. The Moores, who came from Ontario, had nice clothes for all seasons.

Eaton's catalogue was our fashion sheet – Fall, Winter, Spring and Summer issues. Afterwards they would be found in the little outhouse. Of course, everyone would try to pick out the soft pages first.

AFTER THE CPR SECTION WAS MADE AT COLONSAY, THE FOREMAN, an Englishman named Mr Borman, wanted to board with us, and finally Mum decided to board the other eight or ten on the gang as well. That meant feeding fifteen to eighteen people, every day. The men slept in a bunk car and came to our shack for breakfast and supper, and we gave them a packed lunch of cheese, egg or canned salmon sandwiches. Some of them, like Dad, just took a big hunk of bread with a chunk of butter and cheese, and cut it themselves with pocket knives. Dad said that way it didn't dry out.

Mr Borman and Fred Rosher, who also worked on the railway, wanted to sleep at our place, not in the bunk car with the men, so Mum got more ticking and we stuffed it with hay and put it on the living room floor every night. This had to be got up and put on Mum and Dad's bed for the day before the men came in for breakfast at seven or seven-thirty every morning. For breakfast there was a big pot of oatmeal porridge (not refined stuff: we got it in five or ten-pound bags), mashed potato and turnip fried up, and mostly a big pan of fried egg, and bread and butter. There was always lots of milk, butter and eggs from the farmers. The farm ladies sold most of the butter they made. Sometimes we got it in exchange for homemade bread. We baked about fourteen loaves every day. Our hundred-pound sack of flour sat in one end of the kitchen to keep warm. Yeast cakes were bought in round boxes, six to a carton; we made our own yeast by mixing these and potato water a day or two beforehand, and you could use part or all of it. Then we made bread. We made a batch each morning when we had the railway men, and if we were selling some, Mum started the first batch about 7am. Then I would make the second batch about 11am. While one baked, the other was rising. On Saturday, we always made two batches. We sold some to the bachelors around, In fact, we could not make enough. Ah, the delicious smell of newly-baked bread in that small shack! Not so that of turnip or onions cooking in a small house.

We didn't bake so much in very hot weather. The house was too small and had only the one door. And if the least wind got up, the dust would blow like everything.

Our shack in Colonsay was built on prairie land, so the plagues of mosquitoes were terrific, and they sure went for us green Englishmen. We had to use vinegar and baking soda to try to keep them off, and finally we had to wrap newspapers around our legs inside our stockings and get on with the work.

We made pies, six at a time, of dried apple rings, raisins, or jam, and usually boiled a ham for supper, as you could get very little other meat at first. Salted or fresh pork was almost all there was; the farmers had only a milk cow or two. Some had horses for farm work, but most used oxen, and a few kept chickens. Later, in the summer of 1908, when Smith's butcher shop opened, more beef came. In the fall we could sometimes get an old hen or rooster and make a huge pot of stew with dumplings on top. That sure was good. There were always plenty of turnips and spuds to go with the meat, and in the autumn, lots of vegetables like carrots and cabbages, and more fruit from Saskatoon. We always had some apple rings boiled to make fruit for the men. For desserts, we also gave them milk puddings – rice pudding, tapioca, custard – sometimes a boiled one, a spotted dick, or a jam roll, or fruit: CPR strawberries, prunes, home-canned fruit, delicious wild strawberries, when they came out, with cake, and as a special treat, lemon pie.

Some of the men were rough and untidy, and they all got very dirty at work, but we liked and got along well with all. There were several Polish men on the section gang, and one night when they saw the steamed pudding we had made for dessert, they drew back from the table, saying *"Niedobra!"*, not okay, and left. I guess they just didn't know what it was. Not many of the men who worked on the section joined in the sports, but Mr Borman, the first boss, was into everything. He was a jolly sport, and did all he could to help Dad when he boarded with us.

We boarded men as much for the money as anything. You did everything you could to make a bit of money. For people who'd never owed money on anything before, owing one hundred dollars for their house was a burden.

When the Peebles' boarding house was completed in June or July, Mrs Peebles came over and asked if I could help with noon meals when they were busy. When she sent over for me, I would put on a clean pinafore with frills on the shoulders, brush up my hair and hurry over to lay the big, long dining table. Then, when the men came in to eat, and it was mostly CPR construction gangs, I helped dish up vegetables, which were mainly potatoes, turnips and carrots, and made sure there was plenty of tea and water.

Mrs Peebles was a very good cook; she made lovely cakes and cookies too. We served the men roast beef or pork, and often chicken, and desserts of milk pudding, rice, tapioca, custard and mostly pies – apple, raisin, lemon or custard. It was a treat when we got canned tomatoes, apples and oranges. Then after the meal, I had to wash dishes and tidy up. I could only help at noon meals as I had to be home to help when our men had supper at six-thirty or seven, depending on how far they were on the section and the work. Sometimes they were quite late.

Later in 1908, the section men decided to board themselves in the bunk car, so we were not so rushed.

In the fall of 1908, a young English woman named Miss Boazman came to live with her two brothers who had a farm. She'd been taught to cook by the cook at home, but to feed eighteen or twenty thrashers working on the harvest was some job, so Mum let me go and help her. We each made a big water bucket of pastry and baked in the terrific heat in a small shack. The men sat outside to eat.

That winter, Miss Boazman's brothers tried making their own bread. They mixed dough in a water bucket and put it in the bed with them to keep it warm. The next morning, instead of bread, they had nice doughy feet and bed.

ONE DAY AT MRS PEEBLES', I WAS CLEARING THE DINNER TABLE when a train crew came in, engineer, fireman and crew, all black with soot. I was only fourteen, and engine crews covered with soot and coal dust were always coming in, so I don't remember this particular one, but the fireman, a very tall man, was Arthur Bland. He remem-

Arthur Bland, aged fifteen, in his hall boy uniform. He emigrated to Manitoba in 1903 at the age of twenty.

bered, though, and told me so when we were introduced a year and a half later in Brandon. We were married on June 30, 1913, when I was nineteen.

Arthur had emigrated five years earlier than us. He'd been working in London for four years, even waiting table once for Kitchener and the German Kaiser, but he told me that what he'd seen in that time had made him sick. For this reason, he came to Canada in 1903, straight to Manitoba where he got work on a farm at Roseisle, south-west of Winnipeg.

When he left England, he'd promised his mother he'd go home every five years. His first visit was in 1908, the year my family came out. Evidently he'd written to tell his brothers and sisters when he would be home, but he just walked in on his mother. She saw him and the first thing she said was "What's wrong?" She thought he'd arrived unannounced because the police were after him.

Nothing could have been further from the truth. Arthur was a gentleman through and through. It was his training. He'd started as a hall boy when he was eleven, in Putteridge Park, a grand house between the village of Lilley, where he was born, and Luton, in Bedfordshire. Grandma Bland, his mother, worked there too. Arthur's first job was to look after the boots and flatware. He went to London at fifteen or sixteen and before he left had become head footman for Sir Edmund Vincent. He was twenty when he came to Canada.

In those days, employment officers could say what farms needed what men, and they could allocate men who'd just arrived in Winnipeg. That was how Arthur got onto that farm. He worked there until 1905, when he decided to take up a homestead of his own. He started off to walk the eight miles to file on it, but got soaking wet with rain halfway there, so he turned back, and instead went to work on the CPR.

I don't remember meeting him that first time, but I do remember meeting him again at Christmas time in Brandon in 1910. He took me home from Mrs German's Christmas party. Arthur was boarding at Mrs German's. She had a houseful for her party, and we were just starting to have a good time playing games and laughing when Mum and Dad decided they had to go home. They had a baby in the carriage, the temperature was well below zero and dropping, and it was a long way home – from 130 Fourth Street to 635 Twentieth Street. I didn't want to go, but I'd have had to if Arthur hadn't said, "Mr Seddon, I'll see your daughter safely home." I was glad he'd offered, because I wouldn't have liked to have gone with someone else.

After Christmas when Arthur first came to call, Mum told him that she'd been waiting for him after the Christmas party. "I had the broom behind the door," she said. I was embarrassed, but they laughed and of course got thicker and thicker; Mum and Dad and Arthur got along famously. I received an engagement ring in 1912 and our honeymoon in 1913 was Arthur's second trip back to England.*

Arthur was tall and straight and knew how to behave properly, and it wasn't difficult to imagine him in a footman's uniform, riding through London on the top seat of carriages beside the driver, or serving important dignitaries at tables brilliant with starched linen, polished silver and glass. Some people would have liked nothing better than to have had those jobs; Arthur got fed up with helping ladies into carriages, picking up their trailing skirts and bowing to them as if they were his betters when everyone knew about the goings-on that happened. Servants were supposed to be blind and deaf but standing at attention ready. Arthur always knew there'd be a war because the time he'd waited table for 'Kaiser Bill', Kitchener and Lord Roberts he had heard them arguing. All the servants knew.

He'd had little early schooling, so in Canada he went to business college at night and took correspondence courses for his own benefit. The CPR started him on 'wiping' and after a few months he could

* "My Dearest Winnie," writes Arthur in December 1911 from Broadview, Saskatchewan, where he was gaining experience driving a yard engine in the CPR yard. "This is my 24 hours off. I would have been down to see you if it was not for the 20th. I don't want to ask for a pass until then or else the foreman might kick. He is such a queer old jigger." Arthur complaints of the "old tub (engine)". "She will keep leaking... we cannot get any steam, but never mind it is all in the line of promotion. I expect I shall be back firing about the new year, then we can make up for all this."

Arthur Bland (fourth from left) working as a fireman on a CPR engine, about 1910. He 'wrote up' in 1911 to earn his engineer's certificate.

'fire'. He got his engineer's certificate in 1911. You had to take the exams in Winnipeg, so they called it 'coming down to write up'. He wrote up that March or April, and brought me back a little gold brooch. Arthur was one man they always said was cut out for an engineer – he loved it. He could never have been a farmer like his father.

THE WINTER OF 1908 WAS VERY SEVERE, WITH TEMPERATURES often fifty below zero.* The sun mist was vivid and across the prairie were miles and miles of unbroken snow, sparkling in the sunlight like millions of diamonds dancing. There was nothing to stop the wind sweeping the snow all the way from Calgary to Winnipeg. It drifted so badly around our shack that we had seven deep steps to get in and out at the front, but it was down to grass around the back.

* "It was so cold in Colonsay in the winter that water would freeze three feet from the fire." Winnie in conversation with her grandson, Elliott Scott, 1960s.

We loved jumping in the snow and making angels. I almost got snowblind once, and another time we had to rescue a bachelor who had got lost in the snow. Mr Beard had stopped in at our house. It was a very cold and bright day, and before he left it began to snow very fine. An hour or more after he'd gone, Mum looked out the window and saw Mr Beard wandering around and around, just lost. Finally he got back to our house and had tea and waited awhile before trying to find his way home again. He was about all in.

Tom, Harold, Ralph and the other boys cleared the snow off the pumping station pond and we had a small skating rink. Miss King and Jennie and Eunice and their brothers and the Shiers' two men all came in, and we had some grand evenings. It was lovely to hear the bells and see the lanterns on the sleighs across the snow as they came in from all directions for a skate. We used to 'snap the whip' – those big fellows sure could make us go! There were often eight or ten of us. It was great fun, but one night Cliff Shier whipped into the snow bank and broke his ankle.

We tobogganed down the CPR cut in thirty below, on a board or cardboard or anything your could sit on, only it was hard work climbing back up. We had good times. It was a very cold winter but we were young and didn't mind it so much. We'd all had to get heavy coats in the fall of 1908, and woollen toques and scarves; long fleeced underwear was a must for the men in winter, and women wore long underwear and heavy hose. When we had left England, we wore heavy skirts and blouses with big bell sleeves and warm knitted stockings. The boys had had bloomer pants, little jackets, bows or ties, and woollen stockings and big knitted scarves, but our heavy English cloth coats, although they were too warm for spring and summer, were not enough for winter.

At the end of the year, Mum had the regular ten dollars to pay on the shack. It was almost the last one, and we did so want to get it paid off. It was blowing a blizzard outside. I was supposed to take the money, but the storm was so bad I said, "Could Tom take it?" He went out with the money in his hand. The wind whipped the door against him and took the ten dollars to Timbuctoo. Poor dear Mum sat down and cried, and we all joined her.

We had many a good cry. In the summer of 1908, when we were boarding eight and nine men, Mum and I sometimes felt pretty blue and lonely. But we always had to keep busy. Mum would start to sing and then we'd giggle and we'd work a little harder and wipe the tears away. "Well, we're all spared," Mum would say, "and here together – and we must feed them." To get meals for ten or eleven men and Mum and five kiddies took almost all day every day, and there was bread to bake too. When Mum was sick, I had to do it by myself.

In the spring of 1909, when it started to thaw, we had water running down the bedroom walls. A coat of ice had built up on the inside during the winter because it wasn't insulated. As the bed was a wooden frame fastened to the wall, the only way to mop up water was to crawl under it. I squeezed in on my tummy under the bed, soaked up water with a cloth, and slung it back to Mum who'd wring it out and throw it back under to me. It was hard work, to be sure. Then we'd start to giggle and I'd get stuck and have to stay real still and flat to get out. We would laugh and often start to cry, and then Mum would say, "Come on now, this won't do." And she'd start to sing a tune old Mrs Bailey sang at Planks Farm in far-off Buckinghamshire: 'Clear the darkened windows, open wide the doors, let the blessed sunshine in.'

In the early spring, very cold but snowless, the father and mother of Miss King, our school teacher, died within a day or two of each other, followed shortly by the grandmother, of a flu, I believe. All three were buried on a small hill on the King farm. I went and stayed with Miss King a few days, and that spring I often went home with her after school on Friday. We came in for Sunday service. One brother, Bert, lived on the farm with her after the three deaths; another brother, George, ran the Beaver Lumber yard in Colonsay.

If anyone was sick, like Harold was with scarlet fever when we arrived in Saskatchewan, you had to rely heavily on home nursing. The country roads were rough and distances more of a barrier because getting around was often difficult. We were lucky with Harold and Willy Peck. Among our home remedies, we had electric oil for aches and pains, and for tooth-ache, hot salt bags.

ANNIE ROSHER WAS THE FIRST BABY TO BE BORN IN THE district, on November 11, 1908, and Mum was the midwife. She'd gone with a midwife in England to learn the ins and outs. The Roshers farmed near the Pecks. When the baby was coming, Mum went to nurse Mrs Rosher and Mr Rosher brought his mother-in-law, Grandma Roberts, to stay with me and the children in Colonsay. The first thing I did was clean out the stove, and Grandma Roberts told Mum later to give me all the dirty jobs, that I loved them.

Mr Rosher took Mum to their house and left right away on horse-back for Viscount to fetch the doctor. He was to look back from the last place he could see the house, and if he saw a light in the window, he was to come back because the baby was there. Mum did put the light in the window, but he'd got too far or could not see it, so when he got back with the doctor, the baby was born, bathed and every-thing cleaned up and okay; in fact, the doctor was pleased at how well everything had gone.

The second child in the district was Stanley Peck, born in April 1909. My mother looked after Mrs Peck and the baby. The doctor this time was a young doctor from Elstow. The third baby, a boy, was born to Mrs Smith, wife of Sid Smith the butcher, with Mum again as midwife. This was their first baby and I remember Mrs Smith was very sick.

There were two doctors in the area by the time we left, one at Elstow eight miles west of Colonsay, and one at Viscount, eight miles east. They and Mr Whiting, the minister, travelled by what we called a cart – a seat across two wheels, with a horse hitched in front. Sometimes it was very slow. Many also had misgivings about how good the medical treatment was. When Mum was sick in the spring of 1909, and I knew we were having a new brother or sister, I heard Dad say he would never let the doctor at Elstow touch his wife. "I wouldn't have him to a sick dog," he said. Edith was born the next March, after we had moved into Brandon, Manitoba. Another brother, Arnold, was born in Brandon in July 1916 but lived only to January 1917.

THE CPR BUILT A STATION AT COLONSAY IN 1909, AND MORE people came. When the freights went through, there was such a lot of smoke. The passenger train we always waved to. We tried to see who got off if we were near the station.

Another grocery store went up, and more canned goods were available. More meat was, too; Sid Smith would do all he could to get some nice beef. He was a good butcher and kept his shop clean.

About April or May 1909, we moved into the CPR section house to keep house for the foreman. But he was dirty and mean, and there was no work for Tom or me, and one day Dad said, "We're not staying."

So in July, on the Monday of Brandon Fair Week, Mum and Dad and the others went to Brandon, where Dad found a lot of men he knew who had worked at Itter's Brickworks near Peterborough, England.* They let me stay over a few days with the Moores. From our first Sunday a year and a half earlier, Jennie and I had been great friends, as they lived only half a mile east of the community. For a little while, she and I had been the only teenagers. I stayed over because her brothers had shot a huge white turkey, six feet from tip to tip, and since they were both on the baseball team, Mrs Moore was cooking the turkey and having the team in for a party. The turkey was good, and I remember we had a lovely time. A lady named Miss Elliott was visiting the Moores, and as she was returning home by train to Elkhorn, I was to take the same train to Brandon. Mum and Dad had found a little four-roomed cottage at Fourth and Pacific. Although we didn't have everything we might have needed, it was the end of raw homesteading for us.

In the beginning, we had to work hard, but everyone did their share. And everyone had a part in the social life. I remember it as a very happy time. We hated to leave our first home in Canada.

* He wasn't the only one. In his December 1911 letter to Winnie from Broadview, Saskatchewan, Arthur Bland said, "I have got Percy Stimpson up here now for a pal... he is that Peterboro fellow. Your dad knows his cousin. He used to work in the brick yard in the old country."

Working girl

Rosser Avenue, Brandon, about 1910. (Courtesy of the Hillman Collection)

W HEN I GOT TO BRANDON, I HAD TO GET WORK RIGHT away. When I found out I couldn't be a teacher, I thought I might like to be a nurse or dressmaker – I liked sewing. But you had to go to Winnipeg for training as a nurse. Mum and Dad didn't want me to leave home, and neither did I. I was too scared; it was a long way. The dressmaker wasn't interested in taking me on to learn because of my glasses. It was the same at the telephone office. I never did like the thought of working in a store. About the only one there then was 'Woolies', the 'fifteen-cent store', so there wasn't much work of that sort either. I was very shy, and just thinking about having to go to work among a lot of people made me feel sick. There seemed to be just no other work for girls.

Dad couldn't find work anywhere for awhile too, but eventually he got a job with the city, collecting garbage. Later he drove the rig for the laundry. Both those jobs paid forty-five dollars a month, I think. He finally got into the Union Bank as janitor. One of his duties was going around and picking up collection deposits, and looking after stationery. Later the Union Bank amalgamated with the Royal. The Bank paid the funeral expenses when Dad died in 1930.

My first job I got through the mother of a school friend from Whittlesey, late in the summer of 1909. She knew of a lady near her who needed a nursemaid to look after the baby. My hours were 8am to 8pm, and I walked a mile each way. I went for a dollar a week. Mrs

Claude Cook was my employer. She wanted me to wear a white cap and apron just like the maids did in England, and after I'd been there a week, she asked me if I would sleep there at night too. I went home and cried to Mum, "I don't want to sleep over there." Mum said, "You don't have to. You went there as a nursemaid." Dad said if I went there at night, "you'll be the one getting up with the baby." I gave my notice after two weeks.

In September, I went to work for Mrs Latchford on Tenth Street. She had a daughter whose name was Winnie, so I had to be called Sadie. Well, I hated that. She said she was going to treat me like her own daughter, but when I saw her chasing her daughters around the dining table with a stick, I had second thoughts. "Well, you can give your notice," was all Dad had to say.

After that I went to be nursemaid for Marjorie Fitton. I was there for a month or two before the baby was born, as Mrs Fitton was in bed the last two months before Marjorie arrived in October 1909. When my sister Edith was born in March 1910, I had to stay home to help Mum, but I went back as soon as I could.

Mr Fitton owned a general store. Their house was on the back of the store, with a sitting room and bedroom partly over the store and a kitchen and big dining room at the back. In those days, if you didn't have a separate dining room, you were nobody. The Fittons had heavy furniture, a big armchair, oak bureau and table, and a fire-place in the dining room. Every day, Mr Fitton wanted one tiny Yorkshire pudding and applesauce for his noon meal. He brought me the apples from his store. I helped Mrs Fitton prepare meals, and I bathed the baby and did dishes and anything else I could. Mrs Fitton used to help in the store. It was quite a big business. She would come back into the kitchen and say, "Winnie, how's everything going?" or "Winnie, could you do this now?" They took Marjorie to England to visit when she was three months old. I cried like anything when they left. That job was one dollar a week too. I think they left in spring or early summer. They were going for several months, so I had to get another job.

BRANDON WAS GETTING MORE AND MORE PEOPLE ALL THE time, but not many new buildings were going up. We were in the seven hundred block on Twentieth Street, and across from us was still bald prairie. There were about three houses on Twentieth and then nothing until the Japanese gardener. He came around selling

The Seddons' home in Brandon, 1920. It was the last house on Twentieth Street when they moved there in 1909.

93

vegetables. Most people had their own gardens, but we didn't that summer. A long way out was a place we called 'Little England' – a few houses with just English people. We used to go southwest across the prairie toward Little England picking marsh marigolds, wild violets and pussy willows in the spring. There were deep, deep buffalo wallows right beside our house, and beautiful violets in the spring, like English violets but with no perfume.

Ours was the last house on the street at that time, and it was a long time before more buildings went up further out.

FOR THREE MONTHS IN THE SUMMER OF 1910, I WENT TO LIVE with Mrs Laidlaw, right across the corner from the Fittons. I helped generally around the house. Genevieve Laidlaw, her daughter, gave me my first music lessons, and I bought myself an old pedal organ. It was 'nothing down' and I think I paid a couple of dollars a month on it. I was getting about five dollars a month at Mrs Laidlaw's. She was a lovely woman. Both she and Mrs Fitton treated me like a girl, not a maid. The Fittons were English, but the Laidlaws came from Ontario – there were lots in Brandon who had. Mrs Laidlaw was a widow; she must have been in her seventies. She had three grown sons and two girls of her own besides me, plus a lawyer boarding. I used to set the table, wash dishes, do vegetables, clean the kitchen, help change beds – all that sort of thing. Mrs Laidlaw was a great cook and a great woman to work for the church. She always let me get dressed up and carry things down to the church for one of their events. While I was with her, construction on Knox Church was started, and I was allowed to go down, dressed up, to watch the laying of the cornerstone.

Mrs Laidlaw expected that I'd go back to the Fittons when they returned. I told her I'd like to, but she didn't want me to. She said it was hard to find good girls. But I did go back, and was at Fittons all

Winnie with Marjorie Fitton, spring 1911. Right, JD McGregor, for whom she worked in 1911. He was an early Brandon pioneer, entrepreneur and Lieutenant-Governor of Manitoba from 1929 to 1935. An outstanding cattleman, he and several associates conceived the idea of the Brandon Winter Fair in 1908.

winter and into the summer of 1911, looking after Marjorie. She was a lovely baby, and I enjoyed working there. I got ten dollars a month and had every Sunday off. One Sunday Mrs Fitton asked me to help out while they went to church. I did, but then I was expected to do that every week.

About that time, I heard of a job at J D McGregor's, helping the general maid. It was a dollar fifty a week more, which gave me a reason for leaving Fittons. The maid did all the baking and I did dishes, vegetables, flat ironing and cleaned the kitchen, stove and floor. I stayed only two weeks, though. I had to clean out the spittoons. The stableman told me, "When you weren't here, I had to do them every morning." The housekeeper, a lady named Miss Hall, was wonderful at her job but strict and could be nasty. She called me "dainty little miss" when I told her cleaning out those things made me feel sick. McGregor entertained lots of cattlemen. Some chewed tobacco and it seemed they all smoked cigars when they retired after supper. I never stayed around to watch. I finished the supper dishes and went straight home.

An English millionaire who was a cattle dealer was a guest once, and after supper he came into the kitchen and thanked the maids for the delicious meal and everything. JD never did. We seldom saw him; he was always away on business to England or the US. He was the one who introduced Aberdeen Angus cattle to Manitoba, and later was made the Lieutenant-Governor of the province.

It was a massive house. The servants' quarters were upstairs. I used to go into Miss Hall's room in the morning to change. Everything in the house was beautiful and expensive. They had wonderful silver and cut glass. Miss Hall showed me how to set table properly, and also how to iron linen properly. She saw me folding a serviette to iron it. "You don't iron linen that way," she said. You ironed it both sides, I learned. I think she gave me jobs like cleaning the spittoons to test me. Mum was disgusted. "Of all the things to make a girl do," she said. Dad said I wasn't to clean out "those mucky things", so that was that.

That was around the summer of 1911. I had a friend named Gladys who was going to Vancouver, and she asked me if I'd like to take over the job she was leaving. She had been keeping house for Old Man Brookes and nursing his wife, a younger woman from down East, who had a heart condition. It paid ten dollars a month.

Old Man Brookes was a real character. He'd been to the Klondike, and they said he'd made quite a bit there. Mrs Brookes was his second wife, a lovely lady who never complained in her illness. He often entertained his cronies, one of whom was my dentist. Gladys had told me to go to him; he pulled a nerve out of one of my front teeth – and then showed it to me! I remember one time Mr Brookes had him over. I had to set the dining room table and serve the meal. I had everything cooked, the meat and vegetables, because at Brookes' I did everything. They ate, then sat there talking. Finally Mr Brookes said, "What you got for desert, kid?" Not dessert, desert. That was how he talked.

In the summer he'd come into the kitchen and say to me, "What you got for breakfast? Toast?" I had to make pancakes and biscuits a lot, pancakes just with buttermilk. They gave me indigestion, and I got so that I wouldn't eat them. I used to have a cup of tea with him and maybe a slice of bread and butter and then go home for my supper. There were practically no buildings between the Brookes and home, so I used to cut across the prairie. It was bad in the winter, with the wind cutting at you and blowing snow up into your face.

Old Man Brookes was retired, an untidy old thing, with something always hanging from his whiskers. He used to tell me stories about the Klondike days. I think I'd have gone to something else, if I could have, but I hated going to a new place and learning new ways.

EVENTUALLY, THOUGH, I DID GO. IN OCTOBER OR NOVEMBER OF 1912, I went back to Mrs Cook, the woman I'd worked for when her Freddie was a baby, only she treated me altogether differently this time. Her husband was a CNR conductor, and her brother, who lived with them, was a brakeman, but my Arthur was a CPR engineer. We were engaged by then. That changed her attitude a little bit. I got fifteen dollars a month.

The Seddons in 1912. The children, clockwise from bottom left, are Doris, Winnie, Ralph, Tom and Harold. The baby is Edith.

Mrs Cook was a social climber, really. They used to have their 'at home' days once a month, when all their friends were supposed to call for tea. They'd have little cards printed:

MRS C D COOK

AT HOME – NOVEMBER 21

For an 'at home', the table had to be set out and dainties arranged and so on. Women would call and visit for awhile, and then others would come. A few I remember, a Mrs Kennedy, and the wife of the CNR Assistant Superintendent were so nice. At the door it was always "Hello Winnie," as I let them in. Some days I'd have to be there, or I'd take Freddie for a walk. Mrs Cook went out two or three days a week herself to 'at homes'.*

I had made the mistake when I'd first worked for Mrs Cook of saying I could bake bread, so when I went back I couldn't very well say I couldn't. Her old grandmother from out in the country was visiting once, and I had the bread rising on top of the warming oven above the stove. Old granny started bossing me. "You'll have to take that down," she said, "it's too hot up there." Well, I'd left it to rise up there all winter, but I didn't argue with her; I just took it down – while she was around.

The winter I was there was a cold one, so bad you had to thaw out the pump every morning. I wouldn't even take my overshoes off when I arrived, just light the stove, heat some water and pour it down the pump to thaw it. To go out anywhere you had to bundle up; I

---

* Mrs Cook took Winnie with her when she went on a summer holiday to Balmy Beach, near Ninette, Manitoba, south of Brandon. In a letter to "My Dearest Betty", dated August 6, 1912, amid the chatter of a couple making plans, Arthur asks if Mrs Cook keeps his "dearest girlie" company. "I hope she does or it will be like a month's imprisonment for you. Write and tell me all about it, what days you can get your mail and all about the journey" – all of forty miles.

Just married, June 30, 1913. 'Been and gone and done it' is how Winnie captioned this over-exposed snap of her own wedding party in her photo album. She and Art are on the left. The flower girl is likely her sister, Doris. The others in the photo are not identified.

wore black tights or heavy cotton over long underwear, and then felt boots, and everyone had long coats, scarves and toques. All you could see of a person was their eyes.

Mrs Cook was expecting. She was fond of staying in bed and got no exercise, and the baby died at birth. She told me later, "I left too much to you." I got there one morning in the spring of 1913 and Reverend Quainton from St Matthew's Church was there. Mr Cook came and told me the baby was born but wouldn't live. Reverend Quainton was sitting on the piano bench in the parlour until after breakfast. When he'd gone upstairs, Mr Cook called me into the parlour. He pointed to the piano bench, and there was the shape of the reverend's seat in the dust on the bench. Mr Cook thought that was a huge joke. Mr Cook was always very nice, and often had the fire in the stove and the kettle boiling when I arrived in the morning. It was like him to laugh at something like that, especially because Reverend Quainton was a very large reverend. There was always lots of dust around because Fifteenth Street and a lot of the streets and sidewalks at that time were just gravel. College Avenue had a sidewalk but a lot of streets above Victoria didn't. In the winter, Arthur used to come and call for me at Mrs Cook's at night. He'd be walking up and down the sidewalk in front to keep warm, and I'd be hurrying with dishes because I could see him. He used to say he knew every crack in that sidewalk.

That spring was all excitement. Arthur bought me an Eaton's sewing machine, for sixteen dollars, I think, and I started to sew ready for June. My friend Emma Smith went to Hamiota to her sister, who was married to John Davies, a man who had worked at Itter's Brickyards in Kings Dyke, and there Em was married to Fred Price on June 30, 1913, the same day Arthur and I were married in Brandon. They came to our reception, and from there the four of us left on a three-month honeymoon to England, five years since I'd first crossed the Atlantic to start a new life.

'If we are spared...'

Family portrait, about 1917. Arthur, Winnie and two-year-old Charles.

EPILOGUE

by Chuck Grieve

THAT WAS WHERE MY GRANDMOTHER ENDED HER MEMOIR. You can't fault her logic. It was the point of her transition from childhood to full card-carrying membership of the adult population, a natural place to put a full stop and turn the page. If she'd been asked 'what happened next', she would probably have said that life became too complicated after that, too full of feeding and clothing children, keeping a clean and tidy house and making ends meet to be of interest to anyone. Besides, she had only ever set out to record her memories of sod-bustin'.

Well, maybe when she was writing her notes it seemed like enough. But we know from our collective memory that there was so much more to her life. It's a shame in a way that she didn't keep going, but also understandable when you sketch in the details, the joys and sadness. The fact that she didn't continue makes it all the more important that someone else does. Because as time passes and every winter leaves a further dusting of snow on those memories, the contours and land-marks of our own heritage drift over. How do we know where to start shovelling to find them again? In the old photo albums, we see strangers staring at us in black and white. We read names – some vaguely familiar, others not – that should mean something to us and would have if only we knew how to make the connection. And we risk, in losing that connection, also losing part of our understanding of who we are and where we came from.

I think, actually, that my grandmother wanted us to have all the answers she was capable of giving, hoping that someone, somewhere would eventually find her efforts had been worthwhile. In the years before she died in 1981, she spent hours putting her memories in order. Photos and postcards were her currency and she had hoards of them. As she went through her albums, if her own sight wasn't up to it, she would ask a neighbour across the hall in her seniors' block to tell her what was written on the back of photos, and then transcribe names, dates and sometimes a snippet of information onto the face of the shots in blue ballpoint, often duplicating – and sometimes contradicting – previous captions.

She told me she slept poorly but was content to spend her nights in bed replaying the memories of her life like so many DVDs. Her mind was active – "I've heard some folks say 'Oh, they're old and just imagine it'," she wrote in the late 1970s. "I'm not in my dotage yet." This was around the time she was writing the notes that became her memoirs, so it's hardly surprising that she was preoccupied with those long-ago adventures. Perhaps she also tormented herself with the what-ifs and the if-onlys that accumulate with the years. Perhaps as she lay in the darkness she did what we all do sometimes and just let her mind drift.

Whoever she was in her private thoughts, to us, her five grandchildren, she was the quintessentially middle-aged English 'Nanna'. When we were young, she was the bearer of hard mints and licorice allsorts, the provider of hand-knitted socks and mittens, baker par excellence of cakes and cookies, babysitter of choice and the first

Everyone's idea of a grandmother: Winnie with cousin Maureen Bland and her children David, Susan and Karen in Lilley, Bedfordshire, 1964.

adult each of us in our own time could accurately call 'shortie' – a watershed in our young lives that she was delighted to share. When we were older, she was an adult who laughed at our jokes, tut-tutted our transgressions, dressed our wounds, listened with interest to our wilder aspirations and with amazement to what we were learning. My cousin Elliott, who grew up in the same household, spent a lot of time talking with her after school in her sitting room. He remembers her surprise when he'd tell her about atoms and molecules and whatever else he was studying at the time. "How do you know all this?" she'd say. She always regretted that her own formal schooling had been cut short, and this made her respect education all the more. It took my other grandmother, who had been a teacher, to remind her that what she had learned to do with her hands was just as valuable as a high school diploma.

She wore her Englishness with pride and, even in her eighties, retained enough traces of her origin for others more recently landed to pick it up straight away. Her manners were formal, her attire never less than respectable. She sat erect, held her cup and saucer precisely, was partial to a dunking biscuit but did not slurp, even when sipping a little tea the 'English' way from the saucer while the liquid in the cup cooled to just off scalding point. She knew treatments for all that ailed you, from the much-feared mustard plaster for a chest cold to foul-tasting, evil-looking syrups for irregularity, real or imagined. She subscribed to old-fashioned ways such as trimming her long hair not with scissors but by singeing it. And then there were the dated English names – 'pinny' for apron, 'skirting board' for baseboard, for example – and pronunciation that added an extra 'r' to the end of words like 'saw' and 'crochet' so she talked of people she 'sawr' and her 'crocher needles' – which she always carried with her.

Her hair was a source of fascination, especially to my sister, Margaret. It was always so carefully arranged; a coiled bun held in control by innumerable hairpins, which she inserted with the expertise of years of practise, all covered with a fine hairnet. "It was startling to see her at night, with her long hair in a single braid," recalls Margaret. And the hats. "Hats were compulsory to ladies of her generation (and indeed to me when I was young) – sensible round ones, perhaps with a light veil, a ribbon or a discreet feather. And always held in place firmly by a hatpin." She wore a bewilderment of foundation garments and layers of clothing that made her feel stiff and swished in that distinctive nylon-on-nylon way when she moved. There was a sense that clothing should be functional and well-controlled, quite possibly her philosophy on children and dogs too.

So much of what she did helped to keep alive her memories of the old country. Whether it was on purpose or just habit, it amounted to the same thing. Onto our lunch plates crept slices of black pudding when she came to stay, and into our evenings came the steady click-click of knitting needles. The scent of Noxema skin cream drifted from her bedroom and lingered days after she'd left. The memory of this scent proved a great comfort to Margaret years later when her infant son was wheeled away for emergency surgery.

We grew to know my grandmother's preferences: car windows up, not down; toast cold, not hot; *Ed Sullivan* but not *Hockey Night in Canada*. She introduced us to tinned whole mackerel that gave us our first lessons in the dissection and description ("tastes fishy and sort of crunchy") of viscera and bones. On a Saturday, if we were lucky, she would take us for lunch to The Bay's old Paddlewheel restaurant for fish and chips. "Just like we used to get in England," she'd say. At least I think she did, and if she didn't use those exact words, the thought would certainly have been there. Never mind that The Bay used freshwater goldeye: battered and deep fried, it must have seemed just like North Sea cod or haddock.

England remained the green and pleasant land of her childhood. Naturally any part of it that she could grasp, she did, especially if there was a royal connection. She cherished memories of the street parties held to celebrate Queen Victoria's Jubilee and the coronation of the new King. In her day, titled aristocracy and ladies and gentlemen of substance were shown respect. One knew one's place in society and behaved appropriately. So deeply ingrained was that attitude that even after years of living in the Canadian cultural mosaic, on Christmas day when the King's voice crackled through the static of the transatlantic radio for his annual broadcast, one stood up, out of respect – at least this little English lady did.

When I was preparing to come to England the first time in 1972, she took me aside to explain English money. Here at last was a specialist subject about which she knew more than her smart-ass grandchildren (my description, not hers: she would never use such vulgarity), and she approached her task with enthusiasm. There followed a thorough but incomprehensible – to me anyway – description of pounds, shillings, pence, farthings, ha'p'nies and sixp'nces with guineas, crowns and sovereigns thrown in for good measure – because she could. It's easy, she would have said, adding something to the effect that if your old grandmother can understand it, surely you with all your education can take in that six of these make one of those but it takes twenty (or was it twenty-five?) to make something else… all this despite her knowing that the currency had been decimalised the year before. Well you never can tell when it will come in handy, she would have said. Indeed: it hasn't yet, but never let it be said she let her grandson leave Canada unprepared.

ABOUT HALFWAY THROUGH READING THE ORIGINAL MEMOIR, round about my grandmother's descriptions of the Saskatchewan winter, my wife, Lynne, paused and asked rhetorically: "If life was so idyllic in England, why on earth did they leave?" Fair comment. If they had a roof over their heads, a steady job and no debts, what persuaded them to trade it for an uncertain future? My grandmother offers part of the explanation with her descriptions of the persuasive advertising of the Canadian government, the letters of encouragement from their friends, and the comment that her father "took one look at those growing boys and realised we had to go." The girls, at least in her story, didn't quite enter the picture. Attitudes were very different. Remember, this was still twenty years before women in England won full voting rights.

The part she doesn't mention – probably because she didn't know it herself – was that times were changing for the working class, and not for the better. From mid-nineteenth century, industrialisation and imports of food had been helping realign the demographic makeup of England – in the vernacular, driving people from the land (although I suspect most went willingly). The Seddons had been part of the drift from the farms to the factories when they left Warmington for Kings Dyke in 1897. But they were a little late: the brick industry had already peaked and was facing tougher trading conditions. Yards had expanded, causing a glut; freight rates had soared, and owners like Arthur Itter saw their businesses start to slide. So they trimmed rates and salaries – and then had to weather strikes by disgruntled workers in the early 1900s. It must have given her father, Jack Seddon, pause for thought, although as a brickburner he was likely too senior to be affected by the reduction in piece-work rates and too junior to be hit by the action on wages – that time.

In Buckinghamshire, things could not have been much better. Locals in today's picturesque village of Steeple Claydon, a couple of miles down the road from the site of Itter's brickworks at Calvert, repeat the stories they heard from their fathers and grandfathers about the despotic rule of the brickyard, which in time grew to become the country's second-largest. Many men were employed by the day and were expected to be grateful for it. Anyone not waiting in the queue at the time office when it opened at 6am risked a dressing down and – worse – being turned away that day for not being eager enough. But the brickworks paid a farthing or 'ha'penny' more than driving a cart, so the daily humiliation was worth it.

Jack, though full-time and earning about thirty shillings a week, must have seen the writing on the wall. Getting a house had been a problem and even when they finally moved into one of Itter's

111

cottages, there was no water – ironic, when today the former clay quarries at Calvert are huge water-filled nature reserves. Back then, villagers depended on a delivery cart for their drinking water.

A letter to the Seddons from their friend H Ferris Pike, written in August 1908, is revealing. In it, he expresses concern for the well-being of their mutual friends in Calvert the next winter. "They will have a hard time, I am afraid, as there is a terrible slackness in the brick trade. Three yards at Fletton and Peterborough have closed."

None of this would have registered with my grandmother, or if it did, she did not consider it part of the story. She might have been aware of straightened circumstances as they saved to pay for the journey across the Atlantic and outfit themselves with clothing they thought appropriate. That would have taken some time. They almost certainly travelled on the government-assisted passage scheme which the website *Collections Canada* says applied 'only to agricultural labourers and their families' – which is how the family is described on official documentation despite Jack's not having worked on a farm since his youth. They would have paid about three pounds sterling each – a total of six weeks' wages at the brickyard – for Jack, Sally and my grandmother, and two pounds each for her siblings, Tom, Harold, Ralph and Doris. Once accepted for assisted passage, emigrants could book and pay for rail travel through to their final destination in Manitoba or Saskatchewan, which is what the Seddons did.

For such a monumental journey and upheaval, they seemed remarkably ill-prepared. Whether there were pressures or circumstances in England that year that made them act in haste, or whether they just got their timing wrong, we can only guess. They had neither the means of amassing savings nor the willingness to borrow money and so ended up in a dilemma of their own making, near penniless on the Prairies. The land may have been free, but how could they not have known that, having finally made it to Saskatchewan, ten dollars would not establish them as farmers?

HER OWN FIRST TRIP BACK ACROSS THE ATLANTIC IN 1913 MUST have been just about the happiest point in my grandmother's life. Small wonder she chose to end her original memoir there. She'd left England five years earlier as a child and was returning a married woman. And I think she must have been pleased with herself too, or more likely just counting her blessings. She had married well and adored her new husband who was the embodiment of an English gentleman. Arthur Bland's status as a CPR engineer – the airline pilot of the era – endowed her with respect in the community and a very welcome financial security. Not only could the newlyweds afford to return to England while having a new house built in Canada, they could also shop in London for oak furniture* and Royal Doulton china to furnish it.

London was familiar territory to my grandfather from his years of working there. Not so, my grandmother. Entering the grand establishments in Piccadilly, Kensington or Knightsbridge would have been quite an experience for a village girl, and was not without incident. A family story has it that a sales clerk in a London shop who had the temerity to suggest that my grandmother was perhaps out of her league received a sharp dressing down from my grandfather. "If this is what my wife wants, this is what she shall have and I'll hear nothing further from you about it."

Back in Manitoba, family and friends were keeping track of progress on the house at 231 Second Street. In a letter to the honeymooning couple dated August 18, 1913, her mother, Sally, writes:

* Her oak writing desk now sits proudly in the corner of my cousin Elliott's living room where it serves admirably as a liquor cabinet, its drop leaf a fine fold-away bar.

"Emma Gilder has been to have a look at your house. They all think it fine only an old cat has been and dirded [sic] on the beds. The furnace isn't in yet. Your Dad cut the weeds down."

That summer in England, full of cheery women in full skirts and men in straw boaters and shirtsleeves leaning on stiles and smoking their pipes, was the first of many happy summers. She became a mother in 1915 when Charles was born, followed by her daughters Beth and Ruth in 1919 and 1921 respectively. Snapshots in family albums from the years that followed show an ordinary, happy family going about the things they enjoyed: gardening, picnics by the lake, a new car, boy scout outings and holidays on the farm on both sides of the Atlantic. The body language tends to be formal, at least among the adults, but the smiles are genuine and confident. It was a golden period. And it was over all too soon.

ALTHOUGH MY GRANDMOTHER WAS ALWAYS THE IMAGE OF propriety, her brothers and sisters were not. Perhaps it was the fate of the first-born, or simply her own make-up that imbued her with such a sense of duty and responsibility. She was always the loyal, hard-working daughter whatever the consequences – one of which anecdotally seems to have been to become a figure of amusement for her teenaged siblings. With her timid nature, compounded by myopia and a lifelong tussle with indigestion, it seems incredible that she found the fortitude to do everything she did. Perhaps 'long-suffering' was part of the role she was supremely well-suited to play.

She was certainly sympathetic to the aims of the temperance movement, whether or not she was ever a drum-beating, banner-waving prohibitionist – most unlikely. Methodist church teachings and the impact of her grandfather's drinking ensured that her home, like that of her parents, remained an alcohol-free zone. While that suited

Meeting the in-laws, Lilley, Bedfordshire, 1913. Winnie wears a corsage; Art is on the right. His father and mother are second and third from the left.

my grandmother, the others must have found it stifling and apparently escaped frequently to the homes of friends and neighbours where they learned to smoke and drink with everyone else.

But whatever they might have got up to, it didn't appear to stunt their growth. Her brother Tom found a job with the CPR freight division in Brandon. He also joined the Canadian army reserve corps and was in uniform when war broke out in 1914. He enlisted with the Royal Winnipeg Rifles, went overseas in September 1917 and saw action in France as a machine-gunner. He was wounded in April 1918, returned to the fighting in May, then was wounded again, in the legs and feet, ending his war. He lost a toe but the authorities obviously thought he'd lost a lot more than that, because the dreaded official telegram was actually delivered to his young wife, Mary, before word broke through that the news of his death was somewhat premature.

When he eventually returned to Brandon, Tom joined the police force where he served for twenty-nine years, retiring as a sergeant. His brother Harold also became a policeman after an early sojourn as a bank employee. He had joined the Royal Bank while still in his teens and had been posted to Irvine, Alberta, as close to a 'frontier' country as was likely to be found in Canada. 'No place for a sensitive young man' is the caption beneath a photo of Harold and two equally gauche colleagues in front of a nondescript wooden shack that was their office. Later he moved to Winnifred, Alberta. Coming second to a rival in romance seems to have hastened his return to Brandon.

Their younger brother, Ralph, took a different route, working in Brandon's Prince Edward Hotel in a number of positions, including bellboy and barman. He later worked as a travelling salesman for a food company. Somewhere along the way he developed an interest in taxidermy and for many years kept family members in lamps and glassy-eyed ornaments made from birds or animal parts.

Doris also worked at the Prince Edward. She was the elevator operator for many years until she was replaced by a man and became a waitress. Later she worked at Eaton's as a seamstress. Always the sister who turned heads, Doris also modelled dresses and shoes, often

Winnie's siblings on their front door step, summer 1914. A very dapper Tom looks like he'd rather be almost anywhere other than posing with his kid brothers and sisters, Ralph, Harold, Doris and Edith.

keeping the clothes as payment. My aunt Beth recalls many a fashion-able hand-me-down from Doris, for which she was grateful in the difficult Depression years.

Doris caused a scandal by becoming pregnant in her late teens. Her mother by all accounts was furious and would have disowned Doris completely, but Jack said simply, "She's our daughter." When Doris's son – who was also named Jack – was born, they raised him as their own. The loss in infancy not many years earlier of their own son, Arnold, cannot have been far from their memories.

ON SECOND STREET, MY GRANDPARENTS SEEM TO HAVE FALLEN into an easy routine revolving around job, church, home and family. She called him Art, he called her Betty. They shared a love of garden-

Art and Jack Seddon, Brandon, 1914. A crop of cabbages helped prepare the soil for the lawn that followed at the front of 231 Second Street.

Dressed for the seasons: Winnie and Charles, 1915, and in the snow, 1916.

ing and had the space to indulge it. Art planted vegetables and fruit trees and laid out flower beds. He had a knack with roses, despite the climate, and would have enjoyed teasing his wife by planting the new 'Betty Bland' hybrid. But if the house and yard were a hive of activity throughout the week, come Sunday it all changed. My mother, Ruth, recalls the weekend routine. "Mum cleaned and pressed the clothes and Daddy polished the shoes on Saturday night ready for church the next morning. Everything was put away before we went to bed, even Mum's knitting, and on Sunday after church you weren't allowed to do anything except read, visit and go for walks – there was no skipping or running or shouting. It's just what people did."

It was a comfortable life and Art and Betty were generous with their good fortune. Their house had the space so it became the regular venue for events that brought the family together. Singing and music were very much a part of such occasions: my grandmother played the piano a little and encouraged Charles and Beth's talent. Up to twenty-five adults and children gathered around the table in the parlour for Christmas dinner every year until 1932, the year Art died.

Despite or perhaps because of their own truncated education, my grandparents enjoyed reading. Art kept a treasured copy of Shakespeare's complete works, and books were treated with respect. They had favourite authors and would give each other hardbacks as birthday gifts, always inscribed 'Just a book,' and signed 'A' or 'B'.

A glimpse of their home life and Art's nature can be seen in a very personal yet restrained letter dated June 1917, when my grandmother was visiting former Colonsay friends on their farm in Maleb, Alberta. "My Dearest Betty and boy," he wrote, then launched directly into a detailed rationalisation for not sending her any more money. "You might not be able to get in to get it cashed and if I put it in a letter and registered it you might have to go to the PO to get it cashed" – and anyway, the eleven dollars she had seemed sufficient.

He wrote that back home in Brandon, friends and neighbours were looking after him with invitations for dinner, and then he added: "I had two lady visitors this afternoon so I am doing fine – oh, you need not get scared, it was only Doris and Helen" – his sister-in-law and a friend. In the same gently ribbing vein, he took her to task for suggesting he might be idle. "I am doing something all the time... and not likely to have any spare time for a little while yet.... I guess you get lonesome at times the same as I do but I don't find it so bad this time as I did last year. Going out on the road makes a big difference to me. You see, I was in the yard the last time you was [sic] away."

It would appear their household ran to a schedule – not entirely unexpected of a railwayman whose working life was clocked to the minute. "It is fifteen past six, the cook is late with supper so I suppose I must go and get it myself and give her a blowing up.... Kiss the boy for me and tell him to hurry up with that hug and kiss. Tell him I have got one for him too and maybe for his mother. I shall have to see about that though." You can imagine him smiling as he adds, amid several neat lines of 'x' kisses at the bottom: "Gosh my wrist aches."

Three-year-old Charles tries one of Em and Will Hare's wagon horses for size, Maleb, Alberta, June 1917.

For all his dignity, unfailing courtesy, manners and ramrod-straight bearing, Art also had a wicked sense of humour and the ability to wind up his little English wife. We learned this as children through the frequent retelling of our favourite family story. It concerned an incident that took place at the dining table aboard the *SS Montcalm* – just about as posh as you can get, apparently. The year was 1926 and the young Bland family was sailing to England on holiday. Charles, then twelve, asked his father to "toss us a bun", and to the horror of my grandmother, he did exactly that. "Arthur!" she hissed, no doubt expecting the captain himself to frog-march them from the room in disgrace. That this should have happened was all the more remarkable because our grandfather was the 'proper gentleman'.

That holiday of 1926 was another high-water mark in my grandmother's life, a time, judging by the photos, of great happiness among family in the towns, villages and farms of a bygone era. The children learned about Roman roads by walking on them, horses by riding and feeding them, and haying by helping with the harvest. It would be almost forty years before she saw England again.

HER SON, CHARLES, WAS AN ACTIVE TEENAGER. PHOTOS SHOW a handsome, confident and stylish young man cut in his father's mould. He cycled everywhere with his chums and was busy with the boy scouts. In the summer of 1929, he and his fellow scouts had been working as ushers in the grandstand at the Brandon fair. The weather was cold and wet and he came home with a fever and stomach cramps. My grandmother put him to bed and nursed him. Over two or three days his condition worsened but she wouldn't call the doctor. This is difficult to understand now, but in those days, hospital and doctors were for the dying. Art arrived home and stayed at his son's bedside. It must have been desperation that drove them finally

Aboard the Montcalm en route to England, 1926. Beth, Ruth and Charles with their parents on deck, combatting Winnie's seasickness with fresh air.

to send for help. My mother remembers being sent next door to the Penman's with her sister, Beth. "We watched out their upstairs window and saw the ambulance arrive and the doctor go inside. After awhile, we saw them come out again and drive away. A little later, the hearse arrived." Their brother had died of peritonitis caused by a ruptured appendix.

Little was ever spoken about the dead – children could be sharply rebuked for mentioning the name of someone who had been there yesterday. It must have been confusing, as if the act of dying was also expected to remove every trace of their physical existence and with it all memories of them. This may have been one of those customs from a more devout time, like the disapproval of ostentatious displays, blasphemy and all weaknesses of the flesh. So Charles was quietly filed away, his things too painful to touch, his name too painful to speak.

A favourite snapshot of her children, taken in the summer of 1927.

Life gradually regained a semblance of normality. They took a family holiday in Vancouver in 1930, recording their time on the coast in a series of relatively formal photos that, despite the children's smiles, seem to suggest an underlying sadness.

That winter, Jack Seddon died. He had worked for many years as a messenger for the Union Bank, making pickups and deliveries of cheques and cash to small businesses around Brandon on foot. Beth remembers him stopping on cold winter days at their house on Second Street to warm up, his big leather coat and mitts stiff with frost, his moustache tipped with icicles. He was a gentle, kind man – especially so with his grandchildren – and at sixty-one must have been thinking about retirement. Apparently he cut his hand and shrugged off my grandmother's attempts to dress it. The wound became infected and caused the blood poisoning that killed him.

As if that wasn't hard enough to deal with, Art's sudden death in 1932 threw the small family into turmoil. He had gone to bed with a headache after hitting the base of his skull on a furnace pipe. In the night, my grandmother heard him gasp. She awoke to find him dead. When the CPR call-boy rang to give him his 7am call for work, the Anglican minister, whom my grandmother had summoned, had the task of informing the yard office that "Mr Bland has been called home." The cause of his death was a brain haemorrhage, probably a ruptured berry aneurysm – neither detectable nor treatable. The crack on the head may have been a contributing factor. He was just shy of his forty-ninth birthday.

In the space of three years, my grandmother had lost son, father and husband. "Rough years," she conceded nearly five decades later. By all accounts, she withdrew from life after Art's death. She took to her bed and left the care of her young daughters to her own mother, Sally, herself not long widowed. Once again she and her mother

Sally and Jack Seddon dressed for the cold, about 1928.

found themselves united in adversity. Sally might have continued indefinitely had not Mrs Daw, a neighbour of mythical stature, advised her against it. "She's got to get up and take responsibility for her girls."

"Bethy! Mama's getting up!" is how Ruth recalls the day my grandmother started learning to live again. Apparently it was all she could do to cope with one day at a time and a year or more before she managed more than simply going through the motions of daily life. If the cruelty of fate tested her faith in the Almighty, the strong support she received from the church and its members would have had a counterbalancing effect. "The church closed ranks around us after Daddy died," recalls Beth. "They practically adopted Ruth and me."

My grandmother's brother Harold stayed with them for a time after Art's death. He had returned to Brandon after his father died to help support his mother and proved a tower – quite literally – of strength to both women. Standing well over six feet, he was a natural candidate for the city police force, which he joined and served for close to thirty years.

Much of the burden of running the household fell on young Beth's shoulders. She paid bills around town in cash, with Ruth tagging along for support, and watched the one-way flow of their dwindling resources. The day the life insurance and savings ran out, she sat with her mother at the kitchen table and cried. Now my grandmother faced the difficult decision of whether to sell the house in

Winnie with Beth and Ruth outside 231 Second Street, 1933.

order to qualify for social welfare assistance, or to keep it and remain penniless: the only subsidy they qualified for was the fuel allowance. She was persuaded by friends not to sell. It proved an astute decision: there was no mortgage and with the house she could earn money by taking in boarders. She and her two daughters squeezed into one bedroom, leaving the other two for lodgers.

To say times were hard would be putting it mildly. The garden was a godsend; nothing went to waste. The kitchen was as busy with pickling and preserving at harvest time as many a commercial operation. Those years forced a frugality on my grandmother that became a way of life and never left her: she washed out disposable plastic bags for re-use for the rest of her life. Nor did she ever lose the sense that accumulating wealth beyond your needs was somehow sinful, or at least unchristian. It caused her some anguish. "We always had to watch our pennies," says Ruth, "so it was a strange situation for her to find herself, at the end of her life, with more than she needed and more than she'd ever had. When she opened her pension, she would say, 'What am I going to do with all this money?' After she died, we found that she's squirreled away quarters and dimes in her old cedar chest, possibly because she genuinely didn't know what to do with it." The irony is that she would have had a use for every one of those coins, and more, in the 1930s.

Back then, she started by boarding railwaymen; she was, after all, used to the unsocial side of that life with trains and crews arriving and departing at all hours. Through word of mouth, others approached her. One of her first lodgers went on to become the general manager of Brandon General Hospital. In time, she also boarded commercial travellers and students from the country. She took only single people after the one couple to whom she rented a room tried to inflict a radio on the rest of the household so they could listen to the broad-

Beth, Winnie, Ruth and Billy, 'the baby that never cries or needs feeding', waiting for the train back home, Vancouver, 1934.

cast of a hockey game. No matter that it was an important game in which the woman's brother was playing. "So much noise" was her verdict on the wireless – and that couple were on their way.

   She finally got a radio during the Second World War, mainly to listen to the daily broadcast of Brandon casualties of the fighting. In time the permissible 'noise' extended to light entertainment and music. Her tastes never moved much beyond that, making her in later years the household's one and only fan of *Don Messer's Jubilee*, a TV programme of traditional fiddle music and ballads broadcast from the Maritimes, as excruciating to young ears as rock and all its variants are to old.

ART'S LENGTH OF SERVICE WITH THE CPR QUALIFIED MY grandmother and her daughters for annual travel passes which they used during the 1930s and 1940s, mainly for holidays to Vancouver.

Ruth, Winnie, Sally and Beth, Brandon, 1942.

They had very little money – their exchequer on those trips was a small purse pinned to the inside of my grandmother's corset – so spent their days in the wonderful shady and green expanses of Stanley Park and its beaches. So tightly were they budgeted that more than once they managed the return journey on little more than water and a packet of cookies. On one of their trips west, the girls persuaded my grandmother to try Coca-Cola. It was the one and only time she did, because she made the mistake of trying to suppress the inevitable burp and nearly ruptured her nasal passages, such was the explosive power of the carbonated water. The indignity was compounded by her daughters' laughter. She was not amused.

During the war years, she boarded service men and women. To her delight, many were English, sent to Canada under the British

Commonwealth Air Training Plan to train alongside Canadians as pilots and navigators at air bases across the country. Those arriving at Brandon had been posted to the base at nearby Rivers, Manitoba, where among their fellow trainees was my father, Lin Grieve. He was a Winnipeg native with roots in the Brandon area, a nephew of the Thomases who lived opposite the Blands on Second Street. He received his commission in the RCAF in 1942 and found to his delight that the smart officer's uniform was something of a magnet to the opposite sex – at any rate, it worked on one particular girl on Second Street.* He and my mother, Ruth Bland, were married in 1943 and set up their first home near the RCAF base at Goderich, Ontario, moving back to Winnipeg after the war.

Ruth has always felt that her father's sudden death locked her mother into a time zone from which she was able to emerge only decades later, and with the teasing of her grandchildren. Her points of reference were an England that no longer existed or was fast disappearing: Victorian, class-conscious and steeped in tradition and manners. Coming from a working class background, her marriage to a CPR engineer – ironically, himself from exactly the same origins – took her into new social territory for which nothing in her experience could have prepared her. So she took her cues from the behaviour of the gentleman she had married. But when her beloved Art was gone, she was left rudderless, forced to navigate on assumptions about what he would have said or done. The ramifications of this were felt mainly by Beth and Ruth, whose attempts at living in the present – something which their father, with his more worldly outlook, would probably have allowed – often met a stern and swift rebuke. Makeup and clothes, boyfriends, dancing, all got the third degree. As

---

* Actually it was two little dogs and a gate that contrived to be open at the opportune moment, says my mother – but that's definitely another story.

131

for drinking and smoking, Ruth recalls having a 'stick' snatched angrily from her mouth the one and only time she tried to light up at home. It was fortunate for her perhaps that she couldn't afford the habit anyway.

By the late 1930s, both girls were working which helped to ease the financial strain. They gave their wages straight to my grandmother who put aside enough for the household bills and handed her daughters back an allowance. All of them spent carefully. Boarders continued to live in the house but the sense that my grandmother and her daughters were struggling to keep their heads above the water was fading. There was time for my grandmother to tend to her flowerbeds and roses. She evidently had the knack because year after year, she took the first or second prize for the roses she entered for judging at the Brandon Fair. Her old scrapbooks bulge with blue and red ribbons among the news clippings, memorabilia of two growing girls, and inspirational poems that she seems to have been fond of.

While her younger daughter's path, after marriage, led away from Brandon (albeit only as far as Winnipeg), her elder daughter, Beth, stayed at home – literally. After her marriage to Gordon Scott in 1949, she and Gordon bought the family home from my grandmother and rearranged the living space to create a 'granny flat'. This neatly resolved the quandary of how my grandmother could maintain a large family home on very little income, as well as where the young couple could find to live in post-war Brandon. They maintained this living arrangement for nearly thirty years, until 1976 when age and Gordon's declining health prompted them to sell and move into smaller, more manageable spaces.

She became a grandmother for the first time in 1945 when my brother Bob was born, followed by me in 1947, my cousin Elliott and brother Ken in 1952 and my sister, Margaret, in 1957.

Four generations: a 1948 photo captures Winnie, her mother and daughter Ruth, with my brother Bob and me cooperating for a change. Bob had the double distinction of being Winnie's first grandchild and Sally's first great-grandchild. You can almost see the halo...

THE 1950S AND '60S BROUGHT MATERIAL COMFORTS AND MIGHT have given my grandmother a well-earned respite, but she was not one to be idle, not for a moment. She helped Beth with baking, cooking and cleaning for the household, and when she was entertaining friends, she repaired to her own sitting room upstairs and did it all again. Baking was a labour of love, except when she left a cookie tray in the oven too long or, on one occasion that Elliott recalls, dropped a fresh-baked pumpkin pie on the floor. Any tears that were shed were from frustration or anger – at herself. "She wasn't a crier," commented Elliott. Nor was she a shouter. The day he managed to break her window with an errant rubber ball, he expected an earful

*The Seddons, all together for a wedding, Brandon, 1953. From left, Harold,
Winnie, Sally, Edith, Tom and Ralph. Winnie outlived all her siblings except
Doris, who missed this gathering. Harold died in 1957, Ralph in 1969, Tom
in 1970 and Edith in 1978.*

but instead found her calmly sipping tea beside a carpet of glass
shards. "Your ball came through my window," she observed wryly.

Her family circle now included her sisters, the widows of her
brothers, and her mother, Sally, whose health was failing. Sally had
lived with her son Ralph and his family and then with her youngest
daughter, Edith Morris, but eventually needed hospital care. She had
suffered for years with a skin condition called erysipelas that flared up
now and again. My grandmother felt her responsibility to her own
mother keenly, visiting her every other day, summer and winter. In
many ways, she was closer to her mother than to her sisters, the two
of them having lived through so much together, and was greatly
upset by her death in 1965.

It is inconceivable that she would have ever considered remarrying, but for many years my grandmother had a special relationship with a man we knew as 'Uncle' Laurie. Laurence Smith was a fellow church-goer, a gentleman – English-born gentleman at that – and a war hero: we were told that he had been awarded the Military Cross, the second-highest award for bravery, while a soldier serving in the First World War. He walked with a slight limp but otherwise erect bearing and was a regular visitor for tea after church. Where that relationship might have gone or could have gone remains as intriguing and elusive a question now as it always was. Widowhood, like bachelorhood, can be simply a state of mind.

One area where she excelled was letter-writing. She kept up an active correspondence with friends and relatives in Canada and overseas, and with her daughter Ruth in Winnipeg – a letter a week though the distance between them was just a hundred and thirty miles: 'long distance' phone calls, after all, were expensive. Some time in the early 1960s, she started thinking that perhaps she might

On her visit to England in 1962, Winnie returned to several of the places of her childhood, including Calvert where, with the help of a cousin, she located the tin chapel where the family had worshipped.

Doris and Winnie enjoying each other's company at Niagara Falls, 1967. Doris lived until 1998.

be able to put fear aside and fly to England for a visit. She did, and made the trip in 1962 via Iceland as a member of a Brandon soccer supporters club. Soccer? Well, she said, it was the only way of getting on that charter flight and the membership fee went to children's sport. It was the first of five trips she made to England in the Sixties and Seventies, each full of nostalgia, old friends, rose gardens and gallons of tea. She became 'Auntie Canada' to the children of her nephews and nieces in Bedfordshire, sat down to old-fashioned garden tea parties with them and in so doing cemented the close ties we have to the present with those otherwise-distant relatives.

It was at times hard for us, her grandchildren, to reconcile the pliant old lady we knew with the rigid disciplinarian that her own daughters would describe in stories of their youth. Certainly she could be stern, especially over table manners, but we knew it was mostly bluster. Mellowing with age, she found opportunities in later years to relax and laugh, partly thanks to my brothers and me who thought it hugely entertaining to tease her by placing things out of her reach or picking her up and setting her down in a snowdrift. Well, it was funny the first time.

As it happened, fun in the snow was behind the one and only time she was known to have worn trousers. It was in the mid-1970s. She was visiting my brother Bob and his wife, Carol, at their home in Kaministiquia, near Thunder Bay, Ontario, just after a snowstorm. The long field that sloped from their house was perfect for tobogganing, so she was persuaded to 'suit up' in snowpants, parka and boots and take a ride. Given that Bob and Carol both stand around the six-foot mark and our grandmother just about made five feet in heels, she had everyone falling about with laughter before she set foot out the door. Unperturbed, she took her seat and glided over the snow a hundred yards or so down the slope and onto the level. She hadn't played in snow for more than sixty years. Clearly delighted, she fully

Winnie proves you're never too old to have fun in the snow – and that age has its advantages when it comes to getting back up the hill. Providing the manpower in Kaministiquia in 1974 were my dad, Lin, and brother Bob.

intended to walk back up the hill and do it again, but hadn't reckoned on the depth of the drifts or her own reduced mobility in the over-sized clothing. She floundered, unable to move, partly due to the snow's softness but mainly because she was laughing so hard at her predicament. That day she achieved the unusual feat of riding the toboggan down and back up the same hill, under tow.

MY GRANDMOTHER WAS COMFORTABLE IN HER PENSIONER'S apartment on Fourth Street, just around the corner from 'the house', as 231 Second Street continues to be called to this day. Surrounded by friends and a short drive from her daughter Beth and St Mary's Anglican church, where she had sung in the choir and arranged the flowers on the altar for decades, she was able to remain independent. This became more difficult in the late 1970s when she was diagnosed with cancer of the colon and had to endure the indignity of a colostomy, which she did with remarkable stoicism. When we, her grandchildren, visited with our partners and friends, we were met with the same warmth, the same twinkle in the eye, the same interest in what 'mischief' we were up to and of course the same delicious home baking to enjoy with the (very weak) tea.

"Sorrows and joy have been mixed through the years," was how she summarised her life in her contribution to the first volume of Colonsay's *Milestones and Memories*. This was also the predominant sentiment that emerged in an interview she recorded in the mid-1970s with a University of Manitoba researcher who was building an archive of English settlers' memories. Her voice on that tape is clear, her answers concise, her patience with the interviewer's political agenda boundless.

The inner strength that so characterised her later years represent-ed an accumulation of experience, a brick-on-brick wall of protection built carefully. Some of that came from her faith, some from a determination to find a positive in the darkest of negatives. So we have, for example, a poignant photo of a mound of earth on the hard prairie, a fresh grave with two or three bouquets leaning on it. The caption reads 'Our boy called home, 1929' to which she has added much later, 'Flowers lovely'.

My grandmother didn't speak directly of dying, preferring the old-fashioned phrase 'If we are spared' to acknowledge mortality. Nor did she ever for an instant give up on life, no matter how difficult it was becoming for her. So while her death in March, 1981, was neither a surprise nor a shock, it brought the sadness and sense of loss that, though clichés, are real enough. She had heard Art's voice speaking to her one particularly trying afternoon. "Betty, it's time," he said. She died two weeks later, in her sleep.

THAT WAS TWENTY-SEVEN YEARS AGO. WHEN WE LOOK AT THE family tree today, we can count twenty-two direct descendents of my grandmother: her son and daughters, five grandchildren, nine great-grandchildren and five great-great-grandchildren. Add in the step-great- and great-great-grandchildren and it comes to twenty-six. Go back one further generation, to Jack and Sally Seddon, and the list of descendants is close to a hundred: one for each year since the family emigrated. Among us there have been no celebrities – though not through want of effort, particularly by today's younger generation – no heroes or villains, high fliers or low life. Just ordinary people, the kind you pass in the street without noticing how they look or what they're wearing or giving a thought to their circumstances.

And still the question persists: was it worth it? What if the Seddons had not taken the gamble, had remained where they were in England? How would those children's lives have played out?

By common measures of material success, the Canadian descendants seem to stack up well. They mostly own their homes, hold decent jobs or are comfortable in retirement, drive nice cars, go on holiday – none of this exactly unusual for Canada – and are able to afford and encourage their children to take opportunities beyond what they themselves enjoyed. But then, the descendants on the English side of the family tick the same boxes. Through the decades of the twentieth century, they farmed, mined, built steam locomotives, worked in offices and tended shops – again absolutely normal for England. We seem to have reached the same point in social evolution on both sides of the Atlantic at roughly the same time. Just as the Seddon family at the turn of the twentieth century was carried along by the common stream of history, so our modern extended family is just part of the mass. Remarkably unremarkable.

History is often portrayed as a Hollywood blockbuster: epic, vast, high drama played out by larger-than-life characters. Some history undoubtedly is the stuff of the big screen. For the most part, it is a much quieter affair, the stories of everyday people doing what they had to do under the circumstances. Of course the Seddons would have survived, and quite possibly become reasonably comfortable, had they stayed in England. But they didn't, and that's what makes this story – their story; our story – worth telling. It's not unique: ordinary people have always accomplished what to us now seem extraordinary things in conditions of scarcely imaginable hardship, on the Canadian Prairies and elsewhere. They're the individual threads of infinite variation that give us 'life's rich tapestry'. "You know it all happened," my grandmother wrote. It did, it's part of our heritage, and we're the richer for knowing it.

Winifred Elizabeth (Seddon) Bland
1893 – 1981

Eightieth birthday, Brandon, 1973

EDITOR'S ACKNOWLEDGEMENTS

I AM INDEBTED TO MANY PEOPLE FOR TAKING AN INTEREST IN this project and helping on a personal or professional basis. Foremost is my grandmother. Had she not made the effort – and for her, it was an effort – to set down her earliest memories in writing, this story would have simply become another whisper on the prairie wind.

Her daughters, Beth Scott and Ruth Grieve, have contributed photos and documents, anecdotes and memories, all dovetailing neatly with the more recent memories from my brothers Bob and Ken Grieve, my sister Margaret Wilson and cousin Elliott Scott. My father, Lin Grieve, added perspective and context. The family network introduced me to another cousin, Barb Smith, of Brandon, Manitoba, a fellow coffee *aficionado* whose genealogical sleuthing revealed interesting detail and explanations about our family. Thanks also to her sister-in-law, Tracy Seddon, for information on the Tom Seddon branch of the family.

In Colonsay, Saskatchewan, Gwen Cam's hospitality and memories made the trip worthwhile, as did putting Sandy Dixon's face to her name and meeting Jim Gray, John Reschny, Blair Holland and Joan Ayres who kindly showed us around the original Anglican church. Prairie neighbourliness knows no bounds.

ACKNOWLEDGEMENTS

In England, distant cousins Mary Cuthberson and Trevor Coddington of Doncaster were welcoming and generous with their memories, anecdotes and family photos. Craig Warwick, formerly of Hanson plc, introduced me to Andrew Mortlock at Saxon Brickworks in Whittlesey, who with his son, Thomas, brought a personal touch to industrial history in the Peterborough area. Also in Peterborough, thanks to Esther Bellamy, archives assistant at Peterborough Central Library, and Maureen Watson of Whittlesey Museum.

The internet brought me in touch with Harry Broadrick of Censusuk; Claudette Stevenson, whose ancestors also passed through Dana, Saskatchewan; genealogist and family historian Bruce Murdock of Kingston, Ontario; and the Hillmans archive of Brandon memorabilia. I'm grateful to all of them for their insights.

Thanks to my brother Bob for numerous photos, including the cover portrait, and for agreeing to undertake the 2008 Grieve Brothers Roadshow ('playing in Winnipeg, Brandon, Regina, Colonsay and a geocache near you...') Driving the Prairies in March isn't everyone's idea of fun, never mind stepping from the warm truck into near-Arctic temperatures along the way to compose a few photos of the landscape, but the GPS provided a few diversions. Quite a few, actually, but that's another story and I'm not about to start complaining.

A special thanks to author, teacher and fellow editor Mimi Schwartz for inspiration, and to my good friend, writer and author Andy Taylor, for turning the tables with a spot of text editing. Thanks mate.

And as always, thanks to Lynne for her patience, support and good sense in reminding me that waffle is best served up on the plate, with maple syrup, not on the page.

While many people have contributed in their own way to this book, the usual caveat applies: none of them is responsible for any errors of fact or interpretation.

SELECTED BIBLIOGRAPY

Broadfoot, Barry, *Next-Year Country: Voices of Prairie People* (Toronto: McClelland and Stewart, 1988)

— , *The Pioneer Years 1895-1914: Memories of Settlers Who Opened the West* (Toronto: Doubleday Canada: 1976)

Cambridgeshire from the Air (Stroud, Gloucestershire: Alan Sutton Publishing Ltd, 1996

Hammond, Martin, *Bricks and Brickmaking* (Princes Risborough, Buckinghamshire: Shire Publications, 1990)

Hillier, Richard, *Clay That Burns* (London: London Brick Company, 1981)

Milestones and Memories: Colonsay RM, Volumes 1 and 2 (Colonsay, Saskatchewan: Colonsay History Book committee, 1967 and 2005)

Millennium Memories of Whittlesey, Volumes 1 and 5 (Whittlesey, Cambridgeshire: Whittlesey Society)

Rayner, Pamela, *Calvert: Those were the days* (Milton Keynes: Pamela Rayner, 1995)

Williams, Margaret, *Arthur Itter: God's Knight-Errant* (London: The Religious Tract Society, 1936)